# ARIZONA'S ROCK ART
## GUIDE TO ROCK ART SITES

ROBIN SCOTT BICKNELL

www.books.by/rockinrobin

Copyright © 2009 revised 2024

By: Robin Scott Bicknell

All rights reserved. No part of this book may be reproduced in any form nor be stored in a retrieval system nor transmitted by any means either electronically, mechanically, or by photocopy, or by scanning, or by recording or otherwise, without the prior written permission of the author.

All photographs are by the author unless so noted in caption.

Front Cover:
Canyon De Chelly, Northern Arizona
Background Cover Image © 2009 Jupiter Images. Corporation. All rights reserved - used with permission.

Back Cover:
Robin Scott Bicknell

Design & Layout:
Myrna Bicknell

Editing:
Benjamin C. Altenbrandt

V3.0 R1.1

The Publisher, Author, Editor and all other persons directly or indirectly involved with this book or publication, assume no responsibility or liability for any accident, bodily injury, loss of life or property that could occur by individuals or groups using this book. In no way whatsoever does this book grant permission to trespass on any land, public or private, at anytime, anywhere.

books.by/rockinrobin

ingramsparks.com

ISBN: 979-8-989870-4

Library of Congress Control Number: 2008940605

PRINTED IN THE UNITED STATES OF AMERICA

# Arizona Map Locator

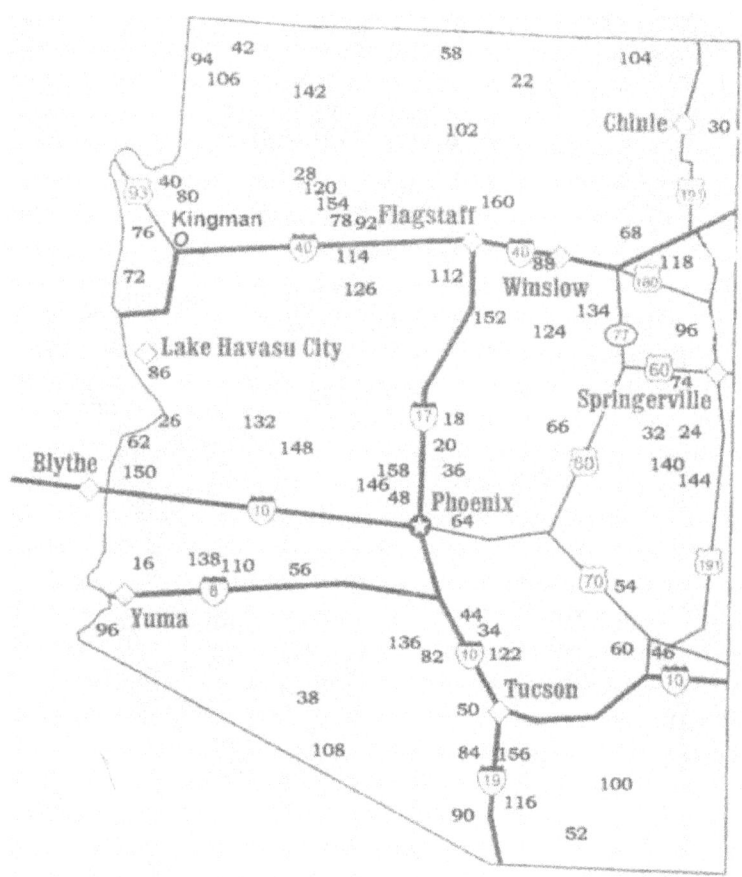

# Contents

Arizona Map Locator ................................................. iii
Dedication ................................................................ vii
Acknowledgements ................................................... 1
Introduction .............................................................. 2
    *What is Rock Art?* ................................................ 3
    *What is the meaning of Rock Art?* ...................... 4
    *Advice for rock art hunters* ................................. 4
    *Some essentials to carry* ..................................... 5
    *Photographic Tips* ............................................... 6

Laws ........................................................................... 8
Rock Art Etiquette ................................................... 10
Native American Early Cultures ............................ 11

**Start of Rock Art Sites**

Antelope Hill ........................................................... 16
Aqua Fria National Monument ............................. 18
Badger Springs ........................................................ 20
Betatakin Trail ........................................................ 22
Blue River Crossing ............................................... 24
Bouse Fisherman .................................................... 26
Bright Angel Trail .................................................. 28
Canyon De Chelly .................................................. 30
Casa Malpais ........................................................... 32
Catalina Petroglyph ................................................ 34
Cave Creek .............................................................. 36
Charlie Bell Pass .................................................... 38
Chloride Rock Art .................................................. 40
Clam Shell ............................................................... 42
Council Rocks ........................................................ 44
Dankworth State Park ............................................ 46
Deer Valley ............................................................. 48
Desert Museum ....................................................... 50

Fort Huachuca Pictographs ................................... 52
Gila Box .................................................................. 54
Gilespi Dam .......................................................... 56
Glen Canyon River ............................................... 58
Graham County Museum ..................................... 60
Harcuvar ................................................................ 62
Hieroglyphic Canyon ............................................ 64
Hieroglyphic Point ................................................ 66
Homolovi Ruins .................................................... 68
Inscription Rock ................................................... 72
K5 High Country Adventures ............................. 74
Katherine's Landing .............................................. 76
Keyhole Sink Trail ................................................ 78
Kingman Petroglyphs ............................................ 80
Kings Canyon ........................................................ 82
Kitt Observatory ................................................... 84
Lake Havasu City .................................................. 86
Lake Mc Hood Park .............................................. 88
Las Guijas Site ...................................................... 90
Law Spring's ......................................................... 92
Little Black Mountain ........................................... 94
Lyman Lake State Park ......................................... 96
Martinez Lake ....................................................... 98
Millville Petroglyph ............................................ 100
Moenkopi Petroglyphs ........................................ 102
Monument Valley ................................................ 104
Nampaweap Petroglyphs ..................................... 106
Organ Pipe National Monument ......................... 108
Painted Rock ....................................................... 110
Palatki ................................................................. 112
Partridge Creek ................................................... 114
Patagonia State Park ........................................... 116
Petrified Forest .................................................... 118
Phantom Ranch ................................................... 120
Picture Rocks ...................................................... 122
Polimana Pictographs .......................................... 124

Prescott Lakes ........................................................ 126
Robson's Mining.....closed ................................... 132
Rock Art Canyon Ranch ....................................... 134
Saguaro National Monument ................................ 136
Sears Point ............................................................ 138
Sipe Wilderness .................................................... 140
Snake Gulch .......................................................... 142
South Fork ............................................................. 144
South Mountain ..................................................... 146
Stanton Mining Town ........................................... 148
Tyson Wells .......................................................... 150
V-Bar-V Ranch ..................................................... 152
Watch Tower ......................................................... 154
Whipple Observatory ............................................ 156
White Tanks Regional Park .................................. 158
Wupatki National Monument ............................... 160

Bibliography ......................................................... 162
Glossary ................................................................ 166
Resources .............................................................. 170
Cities and Towns ................................................... 176
About the Author  ................................................. 178
Book Reviews ....................................................... 181

**This book is dedicated to:**

My wife Myrna,
without her unfailing support and encouragement,
this book never would have been written.

My mother Etta Bicknell, for her loving support.

In memory of:

My brother David Russell, who loved searching for
Rock Art with me when he could and to my father
Robert H. Bicknell, who encouraged me to follow
my dreams.

Last but not least, to my best friend and companion

Trapper Lee

*July 15, 1993 – Sept 19, 2005*

# CHANGES HAPPEN

While the rock art sites themselves have largely remained untouched, the journey to access them can be quite different. We provide detailed directions to guide you, but local government actions and city developments can introduce unexpected changes.

Due to some closures and phone change as well as addresses, we try and point you in the right direction. It is always good to talk to locals sometime they have other areas you can explore.
Enjoy the Outdoors!

**DIRECTIONS MAY VARY DUE TO THESE CIRCUMSTANCES.**

# Acknowledgments

Native Americans of Arizona
Arizona Highways   Arizona State Parks
Arizona State University
Bureau of Land Management
Chamber of Commerce Arizona
Department of the Interior
Deer Valley Rock Art Center
Forest Service   Game and Fish
Grand Canyon Park Rangers
Heard Museum   Museum of Northern Arizona
National Park Service
Northern Arizona University
Private Ranch Owners
Regional Parks   State Trust Land
Wildlife Refuge System

Without their continued efforts to protect and preserve these rapidly vanishing sites, this book would not be possible.
Take advantage of he Arizona State Parks Awareness Program available every March.
This is a great way to get involved and enjoy personal tours.

**For a brochure, contact:**
Arizona State Parks
**State Historic Preservation Office**
1300 W. Washington
Phoenix, AZ 85007

www.azstateparks.com

**A special thanks to my friend Ben Altenbrandt for all of his help in editing this book.**

# Introduction

In every corner of the world we find evidence of past cultures expressed in paintings, etchings, or rock art – mysterious figures and colors painted on rocks or carved into stonewalls. What messages have they left us? Sometimes the greatness of a people is determined by what they leave behind. Arizona has been home to some of the most unique prehistoric cultures in the Southwest.

This book was written for the rock art layman in hopes that it will instill interest in these national treasures and foster public awareness of the need for their protection and preservation.

I hope this book will be enjoyed for its sensitive awareness, its grateful recognition, and its sense of appreciation of rock art.

My passion for photographing rock art started more than 35 years ago. My adventures in searching and photographing these sites and images took me on many journeys. In this book, I share some of this with you in hopes that you too will take your own journey; a journey back in time to a proud and noble culture whose industrious determination for life and survival can be glimpsed through its petroglyphs and pictographs.

**Happy Trails!**

**What is rock art?**

The word petroglyph is made up of two Greek words: *petro*, which means rock, and *glyph,* which means carving or engraving.

Some people refer to petroglyphs as rock art or rock writings. Native peoples preferred to work on rocks with desert varnish. A varnish accumulates on rocks over a period of time, and is caused by the oxidation of iron and manganese. Gradually this varnish (patina) becomes darker and darker.

Rock walls were pecked, ground, or abraded to create designs and pictures. As the varnish was pecked away with bones, antlers, or rocks, the color contrast between the remaining varnish and the lighter-hued rock was revealed.

Pictographs are paintings on rock. Paints were made from minerals, charcoal, plants, blood, animal oils, and saliva. Various colors were achieved such as red, black, yellow, orange, white, and shades of blue and green. The paint was applied by using fingers, plants, and/or brushes made from hair. Some of the paint was blown by mouth onto the rock surfaces. This method created a "negative image" by spraying around the image held against the rock surface, such as a hand.

## What is the meaning of rock art?

I don't know how many times I have been asked this question. When I set out to write this book, I didn't really want to tackle the meaning of rock art. Rock art left behind by the Indians had a variety of themes, from rituals or shrines to territorial markers and clan signs.

Some seem to indicate harvest season as well as times to hunt or routes to water supplies. Depictions of celestial bodies, the solar equinox, and calendars often can be seen carved in rock. I enjoy seeing and photographing rock art and want to help others do the same. There are dozens of books written on this subject and they all have different approaches. To me, a petroglyph or pictograph is as much a work of art as any Picasso or Van Gogh. To be outdoors photographing nature's gallery is all I need to understand the true meaning of rock art, an art that has withstood the test of time.

## Advice for rock art hunters

Before going out in search of rock art, be aware that there are dangers and that certain precautions need to be taken. Desert washes may flood an area in minutes during a sudden rainstorm and there is always the possibility of running into quicksand. Keep an eye out for snakes; they like to hide out in rocky areas. Listen for the characteristic rattle of the rattlesnake. Leave travel information with friends and relatives.

A complete itinerary of your trip, vehicle description, license, and expected time of return should be left with friends or family. Any time a group is seriously overdue, the authorities should be notified quickly.

**Some necessary supplies include:**
- Water
- Compass
- Maps
- Emergency food
- Flashlight with fresh batteries
- Sunglasses and sunscreen
- Mirror
- Knife
- Matches
- Fire starter, paper, candles; even corn chips can be used to start a fire because of the oil content
- First-aid kit
- Hat to guard against the brutal sun

Hide car keys in a safe place near the car rather than taking a chance of losing them while hiking.

It is recommended that you obtain an extended weather forecast before setting out on a remote trail.

In this book, petroglyphs or pictograph sites are marked with this symbol: ◉ Other symbols used are marked on the individual maps.

Keep in mind that odometer readings vary slightly with each vehicle. The mileages given in this book may not be exactly the same as yours.

The maps were not drawn to scale and are not meant to replace road maps. Always carry a detailed road map in unfamiliar territory

**Photographic tips**

The equipment needed for photographing petroglyphs and pictographs includes:
- 35 mm camera
- Digital camera
- 50 mm lens
- 28 mm lens
- 200-plus mm zoom lens
- Strobe
- Tripod
- Twist shade
- Ultraviolet (UV) filter

When I am in the field I carry two 35 mm cameras and a digital camera as well as an 8 mm camcorder. In one camera I use ASA 200 and 400 print film for low light; with the new digitals you have access to even more settings. I use my camcorder for documenting all the sites I photograph.

Lighting has a lot to do with how well your photographs will come out. Early morning and late afternoon are the optimal times for taking photos as shadows help to bring out contrast in the subject matter.

I carry a silver twist shade to reflect the sun and heighten the contrast between light and shadow.

Many people who take photographs stand too far away from the subject. Fill your lens with the subject, organize your shot, and watch for light in the background.

Remember to protect your film from sun and rain in the field. Follow the recommendations printed on the package.

Bring a pair of binoculars for spotting hard to find petroglyphs and pictographs.

There is no better teacher than practice, practice, and practice. Good luck and good photo shooting!

Remember to take nothing but pictures, leave nothing but footprints.

If you see anyone defacing or damaging rock art please call:

# 1-800-VANDALS
(1-800-826-3257)

# LAWS

## Archaeological Resources Protection Act

**The Archaeological Resources Protection Act Of 1979 (ARPA- 1979):** The 96$^{th}$ Congress passed public law 96-95 on October 31, 1979. The act reads: Archaeological Resources are an irreplaceable part of our National Heritage. No person may excavate, remove, damage, or otherwise alter or deface any Archaeological Resource located on public or Indian (Native American) lands.

Any person who knowingly violates this law is subject to a fine of up to $10,000 and can be imprisoned for up to one year. In some cases, the fine can be as high as $100,000 or imprisonment for as long as five years. Persons who furnish information leading to a conviction for this criminal violation may be paid up to $500.

**Arizona State Parks**
Some state parks have petroglyphs on them and the act mentioned above is enforced.

We highly recommend contacting the Arizona State Parks for a brochure. Arizona has some of the best state parks to be found anywhere. For more information, go to www.azstateparks.gov.

**Bureau of Land Management**
The Bureau of Land Management permits camping for up to 14 days. Most areas post the rules for camping. BLM also enforces the ARPA law.
Web site: www.blm.gov/az

**State Trust Land**
If you decided to visit State Trust Land, you must have a valid Arizona license along with a hunting or fishing license. The ARPA law is also enforced on State Trust Land. To obtain a permit online, go to: www.land.state.az.us/programs/natural/recreation_permit.htm

**Forest Service/National Park Service**
The Forest Service also has a 14-day camping limit and ARPA is enforced. Follow all rules and regulations that are posted. If there is a high fire danger, you guessed it: **NO FIRES ALLOWED!**
Web site: www.nps.gov/state/az/

**Indian Reservations**
Alcohol is not allowed on Indian reservations. The ARPA law is enforced on these lands. Please respect the privacy of the people on the reservation. Obtain permission before visiting historic or prehistoric sites.

**Private Landowners**
The private landowners mentioned in this book require permission to enter onto their land; reservations may also be required. Refer to the individual sites.

**Rock Art Rules and Etiquette**

1. Pictographs and Petroglyphs are sacred historical artifacts and any destruction, defacing, or theft is a federal crime. You may serve prison time and have a hefty fine levied.

2. Do not touch rock art since the oils from fingers can damage pigments that may be thousands of years old.

3. Do not rub or trace petroglyphs; making block prints of pictographs or using chalk to highlight images may damage rock art sites.

4. Never remove anything from a site such as pottery shards, projectile points, or any artifact made by human hands.

5. Removing any artifacts is a federal crime.

6. Some people build fires next to rock art trying to get a better look. The smoke from the fires can ruin the petroglyphs.

7. Do not climb on rock art.

8. Do not be tempted to chisel or take a boulder home. This is a federal crime.

# Native American Early Cultures

**Anasazi - 300 B.C. to 1300 A.D.**

Anasazi is a Navajo word for "enemy ancestor" also known as "ancestral Puebloans." The Hopi refer to them as Hisatsinoms, "people of long ago." These people inhabited the four corners area along the Colorado plateau and were an agricultural society that cultivated cotton and wove cotton fabrics. The earlier Anasazis are known as basket making people for their extrordinary basket weaving work. Their rock art styles are mostly petroglyphs and consist of humans and animals such as bighorn sheep, deer, birds, along with abstract geometric figures, curves, and patterns. The Anasazi built pit houses, and were avid astronomers who used a celestial calendar. They are believed to have become Hopi and Virgin River Puebloan and other Pueblo Indians.

**Archaic - 6000 B.C. to 8000 B.C.**

Archaic is a Greek word originating around the fifth century B.C. meaning ancient. They were the first North Americans to domesticate dogs and construct boats. Living a nomadic life, they hunted, trapped game, caught fish, and gathered edible wild plants. The Archaics used a variety of materials as tools such as wood, plant fiber, bone, stone, shell, ivory, and copper.

Their rock art consists of abstract lines, circles and stick figures and can be found in Snake Gulch in the Kanab Creek Wilderness area in northern Arizona.

**Hohokam - 300 B.C. to 1300 A.D.**

This is the Pima Indian name for "vanished ones." They were farmers who cultivated corn. They built pit houses and made major canals that were more than 30 miles long. They built ball courts and left behind many petroglyphs. The Hohokam rock art style consist of human forms and animals such as deer, bighorn sheep, coyotes, birds, snakes, and includes abstract lines and spirals. Their descendants are believed to be Papago (Tohono O'odham) and Pima (Akimel O'odham) Indian groups.

**Mogollon - 300 B.C. to 1100 A.D.**
Known as mountain people, these people were farmers and hunters and developed pit houses and later pueblos. Their rock art style is probably best known for the kokopelli, a humpback flute player. Animal pictographs such as snakes, fish, birds, and human figures usually painted with red color are also found. The Mogollon people were accomplished stoneworkers and were famous for their magnificent black and white pottery.

**Mojave Indians**
The name Mojave means "water" and "alongside," or "people by the water." They lived along the lower Colorado River in small family groups. They fished and hunted small animals and lived in wikiups built from logs covered with brush. They made beautiful clay pots that were traded to tribes as far away as the Pacific Coast.

**Patayan - 700 A.D to 1500 A.D.**
The name Patayan comes from the Yuman language and means "old people." Most Patayan people appeared to have been highly mobile and did not build large structures. They did build shallow pit houses consisting of a series of rooms possibly, for storage or ceremonial activities. The Patayan

made both baskets and pottery and are known for making intaglios, or "geoglyphs." Intaglios are described on page 26.

The Cohonina cultures are of Patayan descent and migrated to northern Arizona around the south rim of the Grand Canyon. They co-existed with the Anasazi culture sometime between 700 A.D. and 1100 A.D.

**Salado – (1150 A.D.-1450A.D.)**
The Salado culture inhabited the Tonto Basin in central Arizona and depended on the Salt River for their livelihood. Named after the Salt (Salado) River, the Salado people used irrigation systems for their crops of corn, squash, beans, and cotton. They were influenced by the Hohokam and Mogollon cultures. Their rock art style included mostly pictographs of several colors, including red, yellow, green, white, and black. Human and animal forms are quite prevalent.

**Sinagua – 1150 A.D. to 1450 A.D.**
Sinagua is a Spanish word that means "without water." This culture lived along the Verde River and north of Sedona and Flagstaff areas. They were mostly hunters of antelope, deer, and the highly prized mountain sheep. They also were gathers of wild food and dug irrigation ditches for their cotton, tobacco, beans, squash, and corn.

Their style of rock art was influenced by other Ancestral Puebloan cultures such as the Hohokam and the Anasazi to the north.

**Indian Tribes**

Today we have many different Native American tribes living in Arizona. Each tribe has a lot to offer all of us to enjoy. Native Americans are some of the best at making jewelry or weaving baskets and blankets. They continue to make magnificent pottery as their ancestors did. When you drive through their reservations you can pick up some really great deals.

# Antelope Hill

Antelope Hill petroglyphs over look the Gila River. The rock art is on volcanic basalt boulders spread out over a large area, making them somewhat hard to find. Some rocks have one petroglyph on them while others are covered completely.

There is also some historic rock art in the area. The Gila River was a major route traveled by Native Americans, Spanish explorers and the Butler Field Stage.

Several cultures are represented in this area including the Patayan and Hohokam. Among some Native Americans, an animal (zoomorphic), humans (anthropomorphic), or natural objects can represent a family or clan sign.

*One of many anthropomorphic figures found at Antelope Hill.*

## Antelope Hill Map

From Yuma take Interstate 8 east for about 25 miles to the town of Wellton. Take Exit 36 E. Ave. Head north to the Mountain that has an "A" painted on the side.

Petroglyphs are located on the north side of the mountain next to a rock quarry. The petroglyphs are right off the parking lot. The hike is relatively easy. Stay on the marked paths to visit the rock art and watch for loose gravel.

**Vehicles:** Two-wheel drive accessible.

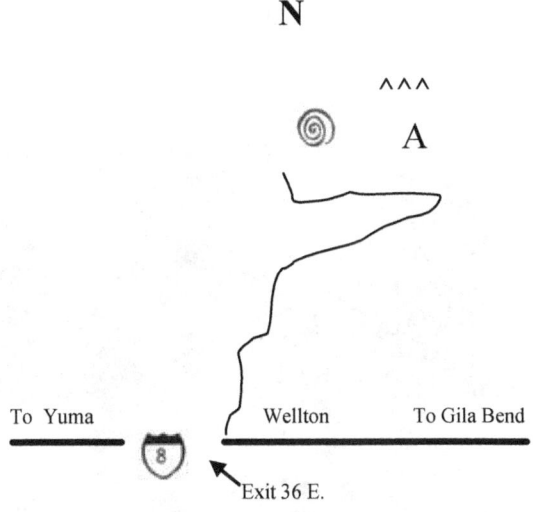

## Aqua Fria National Monument

Plan on spending all day in this area, for there is plenty to see. A camera is a must. This is a remote and rugged area. Watch for rattlesnakes and wasp nests.

People migrated to this area more than 3,000 years ago. They built pit-houses and pueblos on top of the nearby mesas. From these mesas one could see for miles in every direction. The Hohokam farmers moved into this area about 700 A.D. and by the 1400's most of them had migrated to other areas. There are more than 400 archeological sites in this region and more than 230 rock art panels – some of them quite spectacular – have been recently surveyed.

*Shaman overlooking deer?*

## Aqua Fria National Monument Map

From Cordes Junction, drive 3 miles south on I-17 to Exit 259. Turn left onto Bloody Basin Road and drive 10.6 miles on F.R. 269. Turn right onto F.R. 14 and drive 2 miles past the corrals and F.R. 431. Park your car close to the power poles near the fence and entrance to Tonto National Forest.

The petroglpyhs are located about ¼ mile west 270 degrees on your compass. Look for a large black outcropping of rocks.

**Vehicle:** High-clearance vehicle is recommended.

**Contact:**
Bureau of Land Management
Arizona State Office
1 North Central Ave., Ste. 800
Phoenix, AZ 85004
Phone: 602-417-9300

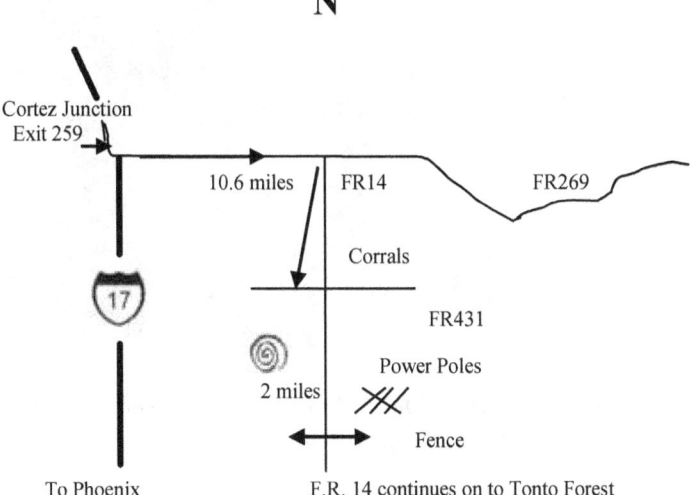

# Badger Springs Wash

People have lived in this area for about 8,000 years. They built their homes on top of the mesas and carved hundreds of petroglyphs on the basalt rocks.

It is hard to believe that people lived in such a harsh environment. The Badger Springs Wash petroglyph site is a short walk from the trailhead.

Once at the site, it is easy to see why they liked this area. The petroglyph panel consists mostly of deer or elk and some abstract designs. This is just one of the few petroglyphs in the Aqua Fria National Monument. This area has been vandalized and is closely monitored by the rangers.

*Archaic and the Hohokam cultures are represented in this area.*

# Badger Springs Wash Map

From the town of Cortez Junction, drive south on I-17 approximately 6.5 miles to Exit 256, The Badger Springs exit. Drive east to the entrance of the park (maps are available here) and continue down the road for ½ mile until it ends. Park and sign in at beginning of the trailhead and continue on about ¼ mile. The petroglyphs are on the left side up high on a large boulder.

**Vehicle:** High-clearance vehicle is recommended.

**Contact:**
Bureau of Land Management
Arizona State Office
1 North Central Ave., Ste. 800
Phoenix, AZ 85004
Phone: 602-417-9300

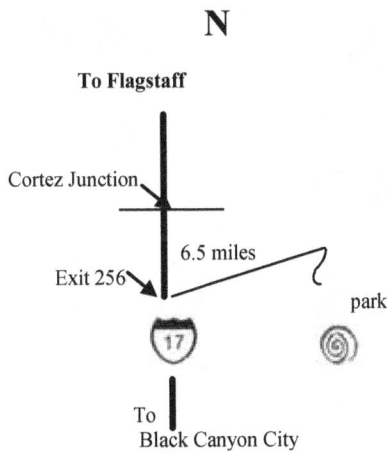

## Betatakin Trail

Betatakin Trail is a rewarding 5-mile hike round-trip. The cliff dwellings are some of the best and most well preserved in the entire Southwest. Plan on a 3- to 5-hour moderate to strenuous hike. Be sure to carry plenty of water with you along this very educational trail.

The cliff-dwelling people in this area only lasted about 50 years, disappearing in 1300. The rock art consists of pictographs and petroglyphs and the paintings are said to be Hopi clan symbols.

*Author's rendition of an Anasazi petroglyph found at Navajo National Monument.*

# Betatakin Trail Map

Drive north on Hwy 89 from the city of Flagstaff to US Hwy 160. Turn right (northeast) toward Tuba City. Drive 60 miles to Navajo National Monument (NNM). Turn left (north) on Road 564 for about 9 miles to the park entrance. The campground is open all year round and features restrooms and picnic tables. Check for RV size restrictions. When we were there, the maximum size permitted was 28 feet.

**Vehicle:** Two-wheel drive accessible.

**Contact:**
National Park Service
Navajo National Monument
HC-71, Box 3
Tonalea, AZ 86044-9704
Phone: 928-672-2700

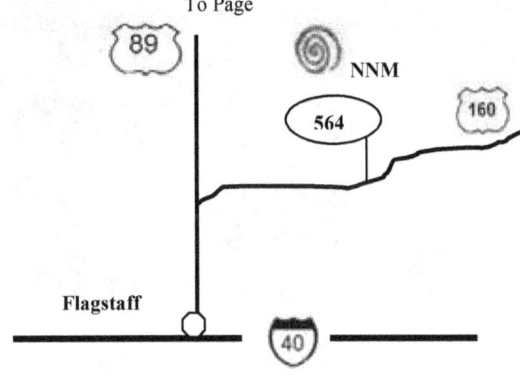

# Blue River Crossing

Blue River Crossing is located in the Blue Range Primitive Area and receives its name from the blue color that is cast in the morning light. There is a campground just a few hundred yards from the river.

The petroglyphs are located next to the campground within a fenced area. An interpretive sign can be found there. The Mogollon culture left their mark here some 900 years ago. One notable petroglyph is huge bear paw seen below. Could this represent a grizzly bear? This rock art site creates a spiritual energy that is said to be powerful and mystic. Come experience it!

*Grizzly bear paw?*

# Blue River Crossing Map

From the town of Alpine, drive south on Hwy 191 for approximately 13.4 miles to Mile Marker 240. Turn left and drive 11.4 miles on gravel road to Blue River Crossing Campground. As you enter the campground, drive toward the north side where you will find a fence surrounding the petroglyphs.

**Vehicle:** Two-wheel drive accessible, weather permitting.

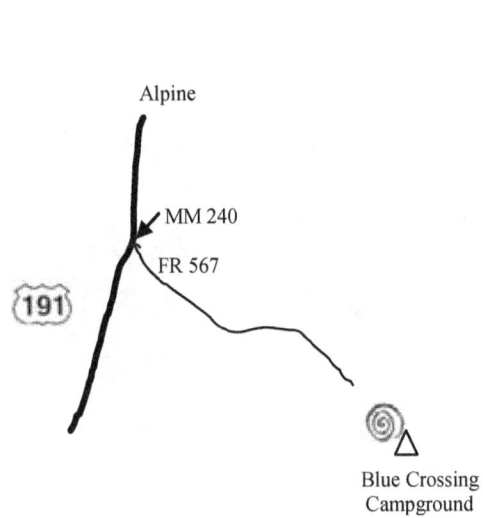

## Bouse Fisherman

The Bouse Fisherman is an "intaglios," or geoglyph. The Patayan culture left geoglyphs throughout the Colorado River Plateau. They are carved or engraved designs on the surface of the earth by moving rocks to the side, creating an image that can measure hundreds of feet long and be seen from the air.

The figure here is said to tell the story of the creation of the Colorado River and the spearing of fish for food. The geoglyph is hard to see on the ground because of its size but there is good interpretive information along the trail. If you have never seen an intaglio before this is a great place to start.

*An interpretive sign at the site of the Bouse Fisherman.*

## Bouse Fisherman Map

From Quartzsite head north on 95 about 10 miles. Turn right on Plomose Road. Drive 9 miles and park on the left side of the road. You will see a fairly large gravel area. It is an easy walk to the intaglios from the parking area. Head north about ¼ mile on a well-marked trail, a 15 minute walk. I recommend contacting the Quartzsite Chamber of Commerce as they have a great map that has this site and many more places to visit.

**Vehicle:** Two-wheel drive accessible.

**Contact:**
Quartzsite Chamber of Commerce
P.O. Box 85
Quartzsite, AZ 85346
Phone: 928-927-5600

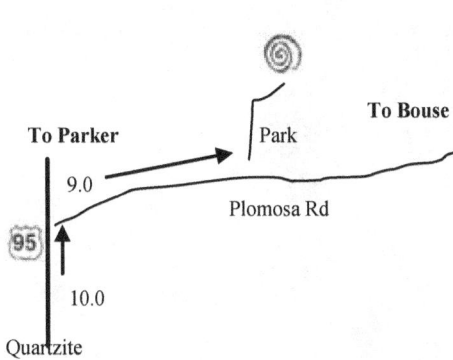

# Bright Angel Trail

Bright Angel Trail is about a 7-hour, 12-mile trip to the bottom of the Grand Canyon by mule. The trail takes you right by the pictographs. If you choose to hike the trial it is about ¼ mile down the canyon. Look about 50 ft up on the canyon wall for a group of red pictographs consisting of a row of very finely detailed deer and some other small animals. This rock art panel is estimated to have been painted by the ancestral Puebloan people over 1,000 years ago.

Bright Angel Trail is an easy walk to the site. Bring a set of binoculars and a camera with a zoom lens. The scenic vistas and the spectacular colors of the canyon make the trip well worth it.

*Pictographs are very faint.*

## Bright Angel Map

From Williams, head north on Hwy 64 about 55 miles to the Grand Canyon Park entrance where you will receive a map of the park and directions to Bright Angel Trail.

Lodging and camping is available. Some campgrounds only allow RVs smaller than 30 ft.

**Vehicles:** Two-wheel drive

**Train to Grand Canyon:** check in town of Williams

**Contact:**
Grand Canyon National Park
P.O. Box 129
Grand Canyon, AZ 86023
**Web site:** www.nps.gov/grca/ .

N

 Next to Bright Angel Lodge

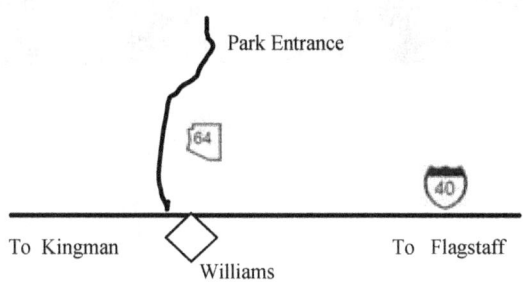

## Canyon De Chelly

The rock art in Canyon De Chelly dates back thousands of years. There is a good variety of pictographs and petroglyphs. The pictograph below represents the Conquistadors arriving in Canyon De Chelly approximately 450 years ago. The horse symbols are prevalent throughout the canyon walls.

The Anasazi were the first ones to inhabit the canyon, building cliff dwellings and leaving some spectacular rock art behind.

*Conquistadors.*

# Canyon De Chelly Map

Canyon De Chelly is located in northeastern Arizona. Take I-40 to the town of Chambers. Drive north on Hwy 191 for approximately 73 miles to the town of Chinle. Chinle is about 3 miles west of Canyon De Chelly's National Monument Visitor Center.

**Vehicle:** Two-wheel drive recommended. There is free camping at the Canyon De Chelly campground with water, toilets, and picnic tables. RVs are permitted.

**Contact:**
Canyon De Chelly National Monument
P.O. Box 588
Chinle, AZ 86503
**Web site:** http://www.nps.gov/cach/

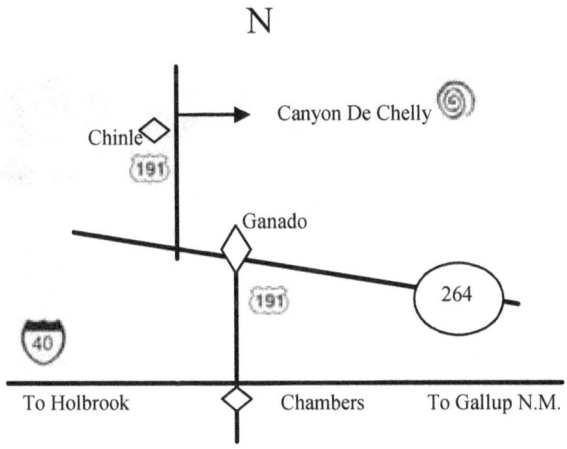

## Casa Malpais Archaeological Park

Casa Malpais means "House of the Badlands," and was named by sheepherders who thought the land was bad terrain. The view of the White Mountains overlooking the Little Colorado River is spectacular.

The Casa Malpais Pueblo has an astronomical observatory made of stone that measures 88 ft by 91 ft., with walls that are about 4-ft. thick. This observatory is capable of recording spring, summer, and winter solstice functions. One of the petroglyphs has a spiral and on May 5$^{th}$ the sunlight casts a shadow on the center, the only day out of the year that this happens. Casa Malpais was built sometime around 1250 A.D. and was inhabited for 120 years.

The Mogollon (western Pueblo) people inhabited this area for years and left behind many unanswered questions.

*Boulder depicting a parrot, corn and a human figure.*

# Casa Malpais Map

If you are in the Springerville area, this is a "must see" on your tour. Museum hours are 8 a.m. to 4 p.m. The tour is about one to two hours and the trek is a gradual ¾ mile and fairly easy.
**Vehicle:** Two-wheel drive recommended.

**Contact:**
Casa Malpais Archaeological Park and Museum
P.O. Box 807
318 E. Main St.
Springerville, AZ 85938
Phone: 928-333-5375
Web site: www.springerville-eagar.com

**Directions: from Show Low drive east on Hwy 60 to Springerville, approximately 45 miles.**

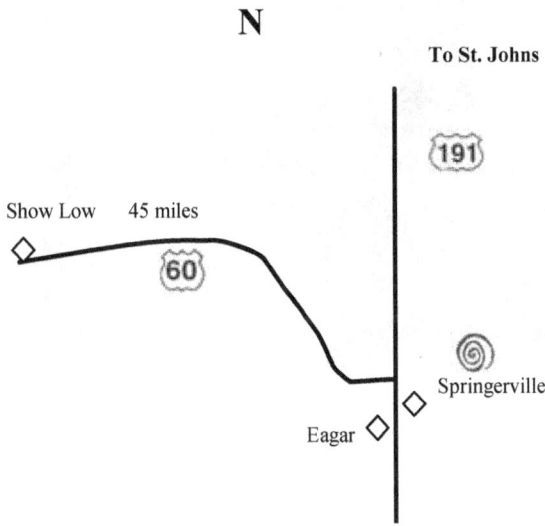

## Catalina State Park

This state park has an interpretive trail to a prehistoric Hohokam village called Romero Ruins. The village covers 15 acres with stone structures and two ball courts. The Hohokam occupied this area for about 1,000 years and established 34 archeological sites.

With all this occupation one would think that there would be rock art everywhere; unfortunately there is very little. After two days of hiking in this area we located a sunburst petroglyph on one rock. Rangers told us that surveys of this area produced very little rock art. Still, the site is worth visiting because of the prehistoric buildings.

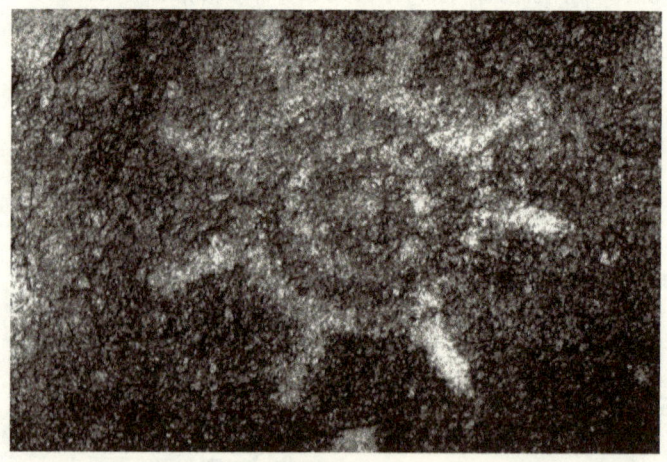

*Sunburst petroglyph.*

## Catalina State Park Map

This is one of our favorite state parks. It is extremely busy during peak season so it is best to call ahead and make reservations.

**Contact:**
Catalina State Park
P.O. Box 36986
Tucson, AZ 85740
Reservation Phone: 602-542-4174
Web site: www.azstateparks.com

**Directions:** the park is on state Hwy 77 (Oracle Road) at Mile Marker 81, approximately 9 miles north of Tucson.

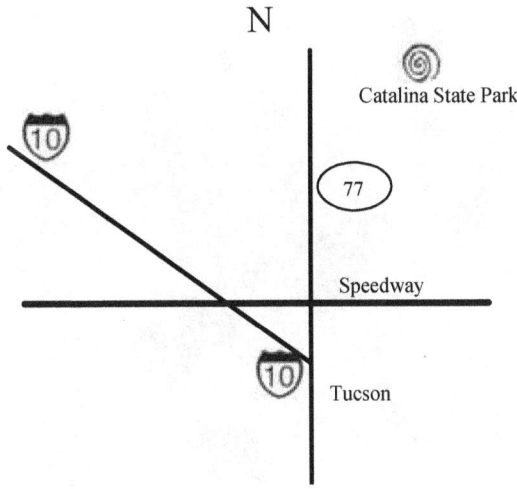

# Cave Creek Regional Park

Meet with the ranger at Cave Creek Regional Park for an interpretive talk about archaeological sites and the Hohokam petroglyphs. Learn the history of the Hohokam people and take a short hike to view some of the petroglyphs.

Recently, a rock with petroglyphs was stolen. It rained the previous day and the vandal left tire tracks, which led directly to his home.

This shameless thief received a $10,000 fine and suffered the embarrassment of appearing in the Phoenix newspaper. Several organizations are pushing for both imprisonment and fines of $250,000 for future incidents such as this.

*Petroglyph boulder that was stolen by a vandal.*

# Cave Creek Regional Map

Cave Creek Regional Park is located within the towns of Cave Creek and Carefree. The park is open from 6 a.m. to 8 p.m. Sunday through Thursday and till 10 p.m. Friday and Saturday. An admission fee is required. The park also has camping, an RV dump station and horse rentals. Call for information on scheduled Petroglyph tours.

**Vehicle:** 2-wheel

**Contact:**
Cave Creek Regional Park
37019 N. Lava Lane
Cave Creek, AZ 85331
Phone: 623-465-0432

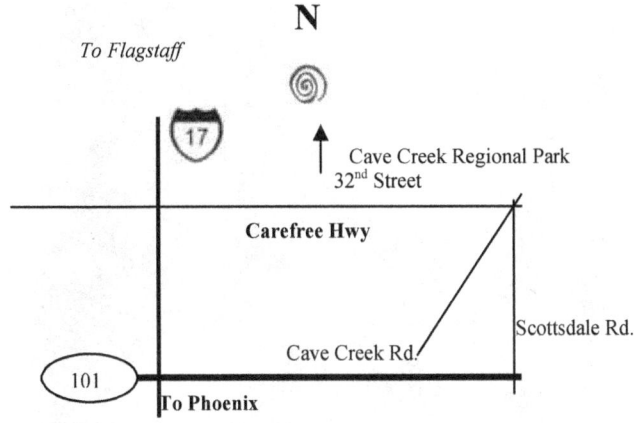

# Charlie Bell

With its Spanish architecture, Ajo takes one back to Arizona's Spanish colonial days, boasting more than 100 historical buildings. Ajo also has one of the largest copper mines in the world.

Ajo holds a special place in my heart because my grandparents are buried there. We used to go there as kids and climb "A" Mountain. Not much has changed since those days.

We visited the Cabeza Prieta National Wildlife Refuge office while we were in Ajo and found out about some rock art off of Charlie Bell Road. It was worth the trip. The rock art here is very pristine. It pays to check out wildlife visitor centers.

*Abstract lines on broken boulder.*

# Charlie Bell Map

The Cabeza Prieta National Wildlife Refuge office has detailed maps with odometer readings and ETA's by vehicle. The road is rough in some places and a high-clearance vehicle is highly recommended. This is the Sonoran Desert at its best. There are many varieties of cactus in this wilderness so bring a camera and you'll be glad you did. You just might see some bighorn sheep.

**Contact:**
Cabeza Prieta National Wildlife Refuge
1611 North Second Ave.
Ajo, AZ 85321
**Phone:** 520-387-6483
**Directions:** From Gila Bend head south on Hwy 85 to Ajo (approximately 40 miles). Turn right on 2$^{nd}$ Avenue.

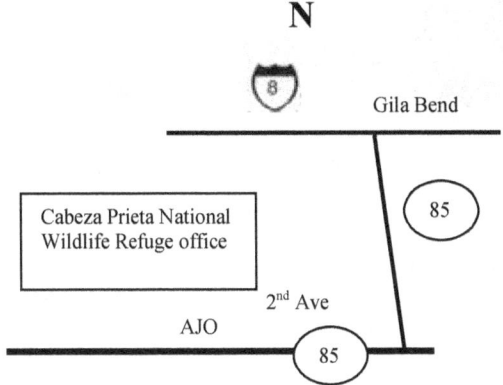

## Chloride Rock Art

Huge rock murals are part of the Chloride site. A now-famous artist, Roy Purcell, painted vivid murals on huge flat rocks in the 1960's. A camera with a wide-angle lens is best for this project.

Petroglyphs are mixed in with the boulders. Take some time to look around for them.

*Rock art by Roy Purcell: (Old Mining Town).*

# Chloride Map

Chloride has a visitor's center. Stop there to get more information and historical data. Head north from Kingman on Hwy 93 for about 20 miles. Turn right or east onto Chloride Road. At the four-way stop, head east for 1.5 miles. The murals will be on the right. I recommend using a high-clearance vehicle. For more information contact the Chloride Chamber of Commerce at 928-565-2204.

**Vehicle:** Two-wheel drive, high-clearance recommended.

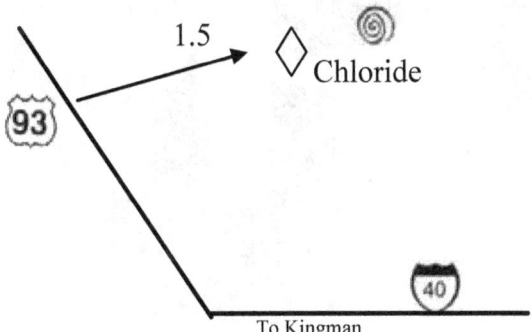

## Clam Shell

In 1996 a local photographer from Fredonia discovered these petroglyphs known as water glyphs.

These water glyphs directed travelers to trails that lead to water. Most of the "glyphs" are a single 24-inch circle with a 48-inch line through the center and a dot or dots in or out of the circle. I met a Navajo at the site who was very knowledgeable about the petroglyphs, and he pointed out a water glyph and explained its role as a trail marker. Hundreds of water glyphs are found throughout the Arizona Strip.

*Virgil Homer
pointing to a faint water glyph.*

# Clam Shell Map

**Roads End Scenic Tours** - This Jeep tour is an opportunity to explore Arizona's most remote places. It's a hand's-on tour to get people involved with their surroundings. The tour includes visits to an underground lake, hidden arches, Indian ruins and petroglyphs. Kanab, Utah is approximately 3 miles from Fredonia. For more information on custom trips and group rates, contact the company.

Roads End Scenic Tours
59 East 100 South
Kanab, UT 84741
Phone: 1-866-656-6664 or phone/fax 435-644-8144
Web site: www.zionnational-park.com/guide.htm

If you have an RV, stock up at the Chevron station in Fredonia, which carries water, a dump station, ice, food, and beverages. An RV park is conveniently located next door.

For more information on water glyphs go to www.waterglyphs.org

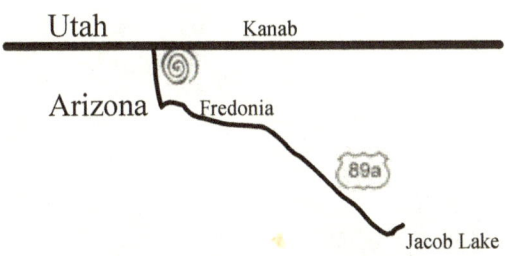

# Council Rock

Just north of Tombstone, "a town too tough to die," are the Dragoon Mountains, famously called "the Cochise stronghold." In these mountains and canyons, Cochise and his people took refuge. From here they could make raids on Tombstone then regroup back to the Dragoon Mountains. The raids lasted from 1860 to 1872. In 1872, General Howard signed a peace treaty with the Apaches at Council Rock. It is rumored that Cochise is buried in this area.

The pictographs located at this site are roughly 1,000 years old and were painted by the Mogollon people. The Dragoon Mountains are spectacular, a place where time seems to stand still.

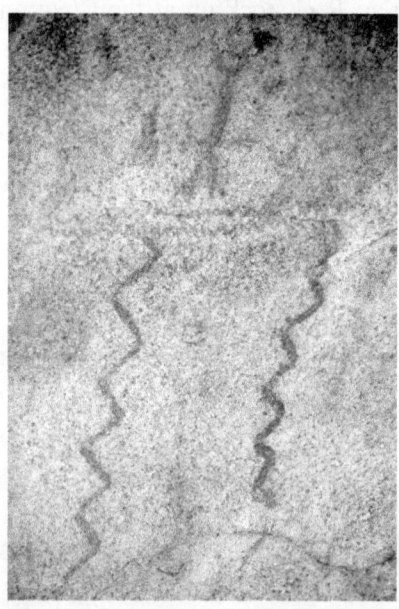

Pictograph at Council Rocks site.

# Council Rocks Map

From Tombstone, take Hwy 80 north for 2 miles to Mile Marker 315. Turn right onto a gravel road and continue for 10 miles to a sign reading "Cochise Stronghold." Turn left and drive 8 miles to F.R. 687 K the parking lot. There are two trails that lead to the pictographs; I found the one on the left side is easier.

**Vehicle**: Two-wheel drive, weather permitting; park RV in town.

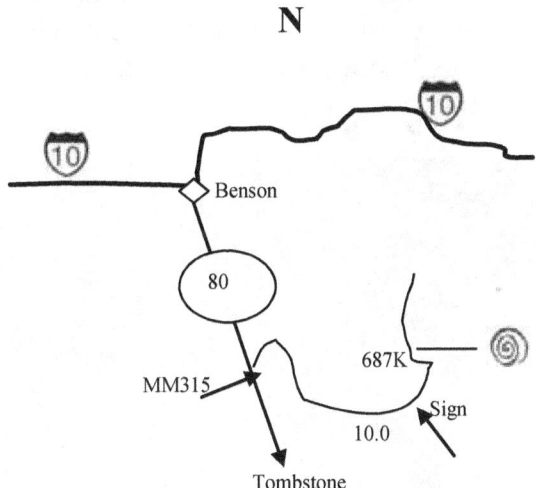

## Dankworth State Park

The Bureau of Land Management and the Arizona State Parks System operate Dankworth Village. This trail takes one back through history to the Paleo-Indians (Clovis culture) mammoth hunters, then onto the Archaic, Mogollon and the

Apache cultures on up to the Spanish arrival in the New World.

The rock art was thought to be from the Archaic culture (8,000 B.C. to 300 B.C.). The rock art is mixed in with village scenes, pit houses, wikiups, roasting pits, and other artifacts.

From the parking lot it is an easy half-mile walk to the prehistoric village, where there are picnic areas, restrooms, and a pond for fishing. This is a great family trip.

*Dankworth Village petroglyph.*

## Dankworth State Park Map

Heading south on Hwy 191 from Safford, drive 7 miles to the Dankworth Ponds State Park sign. Turn left at Mile Marker 113 (east). This goes right into the parking lot. There is an entrance fee for this day-use-only park, which is open all year round. Be sure to pick up a trail guide at the office before hitting the trail. Thatcher Museum, located a short distance from Safford, has one of the most impressive artifact collections in the state. Put this on your list of things to do.

Safford has food, gas, RV parks and shopping. Just south of Safford is Roper Lake State Park with RV parking and fishing.

**Contact:**
Bureau of Land Management
Safford Field Office
711 14$^{th}$ Ave.
Safford, AZ 85546
Phone: 928-348-4400

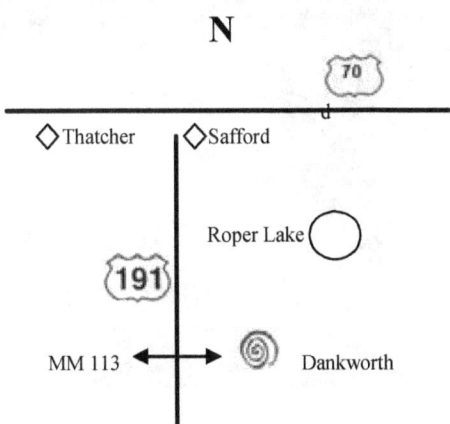

## Deer Valley

Deer Valley Rock Art Center has more than 1,500 recorded petroglyphs on more than 600 boulders. The quarter-mile trail follows the bases of Hedgpeths Hill, where hundreds of rock art figures can be found. Some of these date back 10,000 years to the Archaic people. Deer Valley Rock Art Center also serves as a research center for rock art. They have guided tours and a gift shop with a lot of petroglyph items.

*Anthropomorphic figure.*

# Deer Valley Map

From Phoenix, head north on I-17 for about 15 miles. Take the Deer Valley Drive exit (Exit 217B) and drive west (left) for about 2 miles, keeping to the right while passing 35$^{th}$ Avenue.

**Vehicle:** Two-wheel drive recommended.

**Contact:**
Deer Valley Rock Art Center
P.O. Box 41998
Phoenix, AZ 85080-1998
Phone: 623-582-8007

N

To Flagstaff

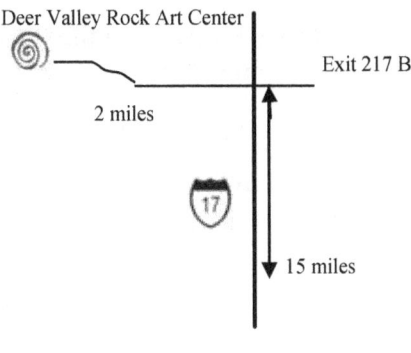

Deer Valley Rock Art Center

Exit 217 B

2 miles

15 miles

To Phoenix

# Desert Museum

The Desert Museum has a lot to offer. The museum is a world-renowned zoo, botanical garden, and history museum. You will learn a bit about the Sonoran Desert, earth sciences, mountain woodlands, and desert grasslands.

If you don't stop and see this place you are missing one of the best opportunities to see more than 30 animal species and 1,200 different kinds of plant displays. Be prepared to spend at least four hours or more. Your family will want to come back again.

**Contact:**
Desert Museum
2021 N. Kinney Road
Tucson, AZ 85743-8918
Phone: 520-883-2702
Fax: 520-883-2500

There is a campground just a mile from the museum offering RV camping, a dump station, water and electricity.

**Contact the campground at:**
Gilbert Ray Campground
8451 McCain Loop Road
Tucson, AZ 85735
Phone: 520-883-4200

# Desert Museum Map

*Petroglyph in front of the museum.
Photograph courtesy of Margie Urquidi.*

As you are heading south on I-10 from Phoenix you will merge onto I-19. Take the Ajo Way ramp exit 99. Turn right off the ramp onto Hwy 86. Drive approximately 5 miles and turn right on Kinney Road and drive 7 more miles.

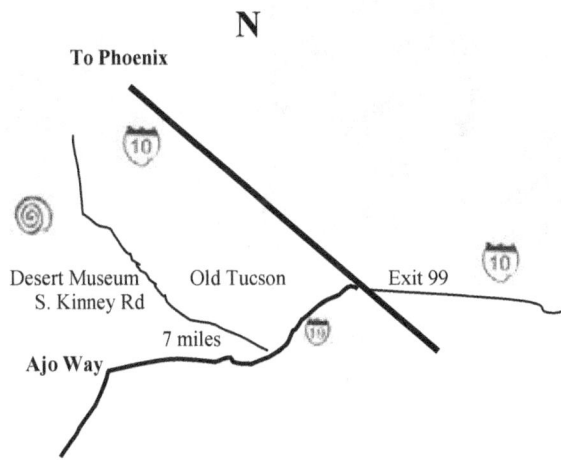

## Fort Huachuca

This active U.S. Army post has two rock art sites. The first is the Garden Canyon pictograph site. This unique site with water and lush vegetation has many pictographs. The second site, Rappel Cliffs Rock Shelter, is located less than a mile up the road from the Garden site.

Prehistoric Native Americans occupied the San Pedro Valley from 300 A.D. to 1540 A.D. They planted corn, beans and squash. The Apaches moved into this region in the 1700's.

Fort Huachuca has museums, the Old Post Cemetery, and golfing. Reservoir Hill Overlook offers some good bird watching.

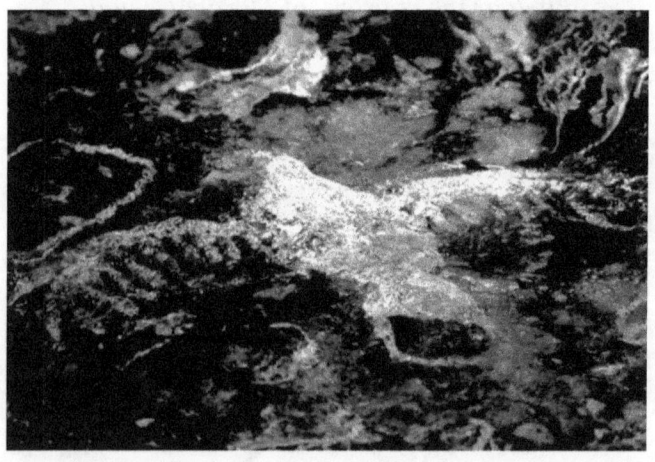

*Pictograph of bird. Photograph courtesy of Margie Urquidi.*

# Fort Huachuca Map

*Because it is an active Army post, entering Fort Huachuca may require two pieces of identification for each person traveling in a vehicle. Call ahead for details and further instructions.*

From Tucson, drive east on Hwy 10 to Exit 302. Head south on Hwy 90 toward Sierra Vista for approximately 25 miles.

**Vehicle:** Two-wheel drive recommended.

**Contact:**
Fort Huachuca/Museum Director
Attn: ATZS-TDO-M,
Fort Huachuca, AZ 85613-6000

Phone: 520-533-5736

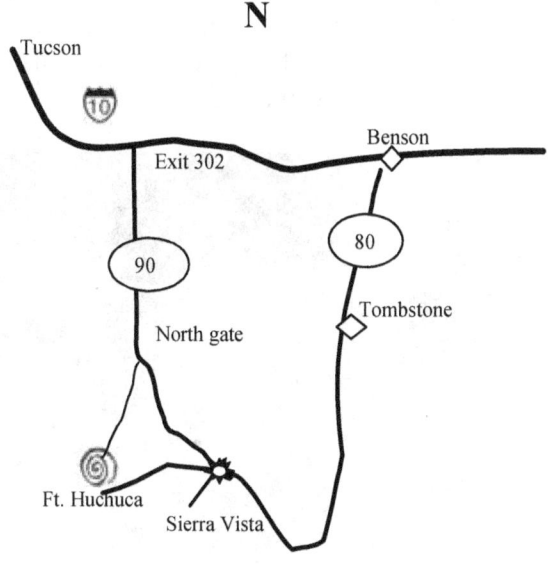

## Gila Box

The Gila River, the San Francisco River, Bonita Creek, and Eagle Creek are the four waterways that flow throughout the Gila Box area. Several cultures inhabited this area, including the Anasazi and the Mogollon.

There are hundreds of species of birds that are found in a variety of trees such as cottonwood, mesquite, and sycamore. On our way into Bonita Creek, we encountered some Coatimundi's. I've known people who have lived here all their lives and never seen one.

Watch for a small boulder right out of Spring Canyon Picnic Area with a petroglyph on it that resembles a horned lizard. Further up the road is Bonita Creek, where there are some pictographs to be found in caves that appear to have been burned by fire many years ago. They consist of red figures possibly, anthropomorphic (human-like), with their arms stretched out. This place is an oasis in the desert and worth the drive.

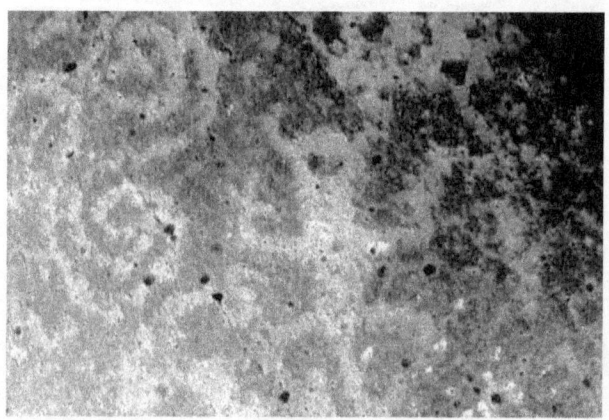

Looks like a horned lizard.

# Gila Box Map

This is a very special place to visit so we recommend that you visit the B.L.M. office located in Safford. Here you can get a map and other information of the area you are about to visit.

Bring lots of water and let someone know where you are if you plan on hiking in the Gila Box Riparian National Conservation Area.

**Contact:**
Bureau of Land Management
Safford Field Office
711 14th Avenue
Safford, AZ 85546
Phone: 928-348-4400
Web site: safford.az.blm.gov

*John and Shirl Tanner crossing Bonita Creek.
Photograph by Margi Urquidi.*

## Gilespi Dam

This site has numerous petroglyphs depicting anthropomorphic, zoomorphic, and geometric designs on some of the blackest basalt rock I have ever seen. This rock art is quite impressive and representative of the Gila petroglyph style, which is found throughout central and southern Arizona.

The petroglyphs are said to be Hohokam rock art. These people flourished along the Gila and the Salt Rivers between 300 A.D. to the 1400's, and then disappeared. It is thought that the Pima and Tohono O'odham Indians are their descendants.

*Dick Tanner at Gilespi site.*

# Gilespi Dam Map

From Gila Bend, head north on old US 80 about 20 miles to Gilespi Dam and bridge. After crossing the bridge, continue about 1 mile. The petroglyphs are located on the left side of the highway. They can be seen from the road by looking upward. Bring a camera with a zoom lens. Try to get there in the afternoon. Watch your footing as the boulders are very loose.

**Vehicle:** Two-wheel drive recommended.

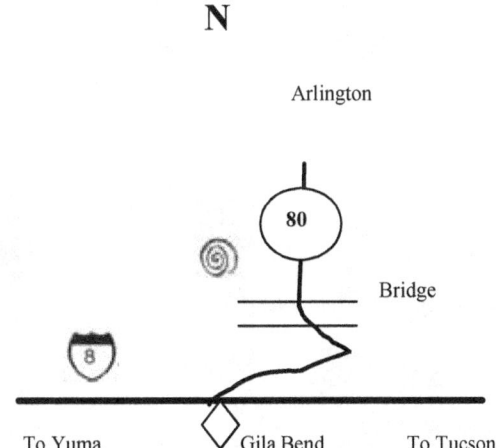

# Glen Canyon

This unbelievable 6-hour rafting trip will have you talking for weeks. The sandstone cliffs tower hundreds of feet high with colors seen in no other place but on the mighty Colorado River. If you are lucky you might see a North American condor.

One of the stops on the way is to this protected rock art panel shown below. It is a very impressive procession of sheep that dates back some 1,000 years. The distinct Anasazi details reveal the work of a skilled artist. A guide is available to take you through the history of the canyon and the many prehistoric cultures that called this place home.

The end of the trip is at Lees Ferry, where you will board a coach or van that will take you back to the city of Page. The half-day smooth-water boat trip is a piece of cake so leave the Dramamine at home.

*Procession of sheep on rock art.*

# Glen Canyon Map

If you are coming from Flagstaff, head north on Hwy 89 toward Page for about 2 hours. The town of Page is located in the northern part of Arizona.

**Contact:**
Colorado River Discovery, LLC
130 6$^{th}$ Ave.
Page, AZ 86040
Phone: 1-888-522-6644
Web site: www.raftthecanyon.com

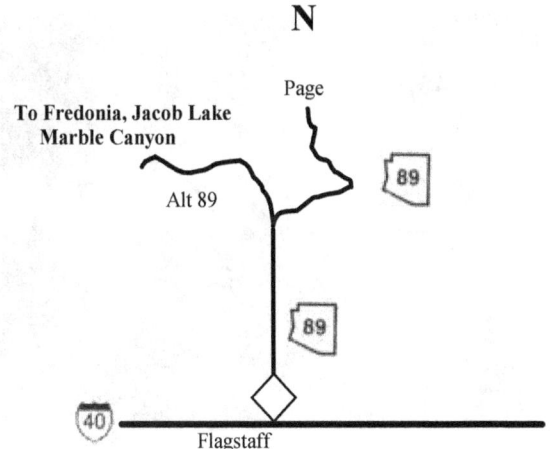

## Graham County Museum

The Thatcher Museum is located on the Old West Highway and its motto is, "Link the past with the present." The museum began in 1965 and is located in an old elementary school that exhibits a wide variety of historical antiques and artifacts.

Two rooms display prehistoric artifacts, some of which are the best I've seen anywhere. The museum also has a collection of local rock art in a few display cases. If you want to learn anything about Graham County this museum is the place to start. No wonder it's been called "the finest small museum in Arizona."

*Located inside the Thatcher Museum.*

# Graham County Historical Society Museum Map

**From Globe**, travel south 77 miles to Thatcher.
**From Safford**, drive west about 4 miles.

**Contact:**
Graham County Historical Society Museum
P.O. Box 290
Thatcher, AZ 85552
 Phone: 928-348-0470

## Harcuvar

These petroglyphs are located on a major trail used by the early travelers. As one stands in front of these etched symbols, they appear to give direction to the trails. There are several anthropomorphic (human-like) figures walking.

In the center of the boulder, a cross represents the planet Venus. The two circles could depict a timetable or possibly two moons. At the top left of the panel is what looks like an olla (water container) that stands out as if to say, "Water is needed for this journey." These are my thoughts on these petroglyphs. What do you see?

*Hohokam petroglyphs on a large boulder alongside the road.*

# Harcuvar Map

From Quartzsite, drive east on I-10 for 12 miles to Hwy 60/Exit 31. Go left and continue for about 22 miles. The petroglyphs are on the right side of Hwy 60 between Mile Marker 52 and 53. The petroglyphs can be seen on a large boulder from the highway, surrounded by a fence.

**Vehicle:** Two-wheel drive recommended.

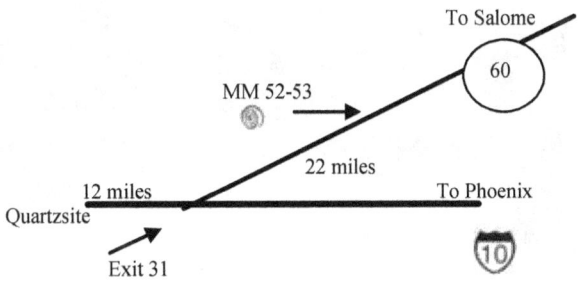

## Hieroglyphic Canyon

On the edge of the Superstition Mountains sit some of the most spectacular petroglyphs. One panel has more than 25 bighorn sheep. There are so many to see that before you know it you may be standing on one. You can get close enough to touch these petroglyphs, but the oil from your hands will damage them forever so resist the temptation.

The view of the valley from this site is incredible. There are three pools of water, which made this place special for the Hohokam people living in this area some 1,000 years ago.

*Zoomorphic quadrupeds.*

# Hieroglyphic Canyon Map

The trail is well marked and the trip takes about 3 hours. We were told the trail was approximately 1.5 miles. I think it is more like 2 miles. A good pair of shoes should be worn as well as a hat for shade, as it can be quite hot even in the winter.

There is a nice big parking lot with interpretive signs and a map on how to reach the rock art. Be sure to bring a camera with zoom lens. The best time for taking photographs is in the late afternoon.

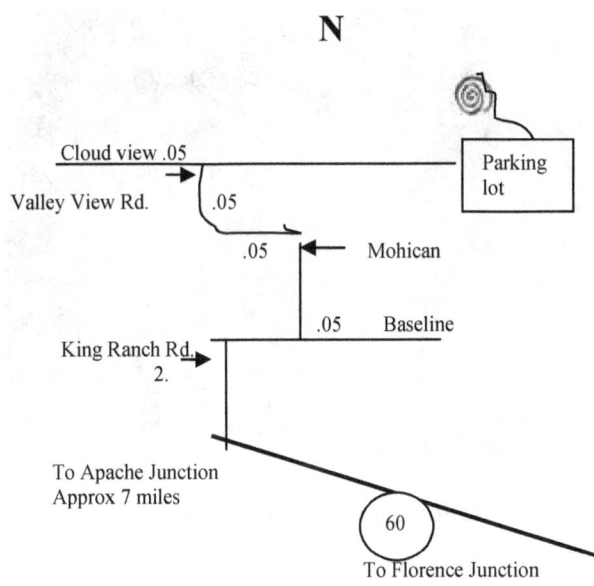

# Hieroglyphic Point

This rock art overlooks one of the most spectacular views of the Salt River Canyon. The cougar seem to hold power in this area. Do the anthropomorphic figures suggest the movements of the cougars are blocked from entering the real world? The Hohokam culture left these petroglyphs behind sometime between the years 300 A.D. to 1450 A.D.

Unfortunately people have damaged this fragile site with spray paint. Easy public access put this site in jeopardy of being lost forever.

*Human and cougar figures.*

# Hieroglyphic Point Map

Hieroglyphic Point is located approximately 50 miles south of Show Low on Hwy 60 or approximately 51 miles north of Globe. It is located between Mile Marker 290 and 291. There is a large parking area with stairs that lead you to the petroglyphs.

**Vehicle:** Two-wheel drive accessible.

N

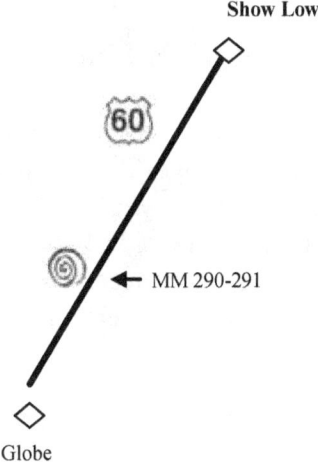

## Homolovi Ruins Petroglyphs

Homolovi Ruins State Park, east of Winslow, was established in 1986. The name Homolovi is Hopi for "the place of the little hills." Ancient people (Anasazi) who built their homes along the Little Colorado River inhabited this area. The park has camping available and a visitor's center for information.

Homolovi Ruins has four areas of ongoing excavation conducted by several archaeologists and is currently the center of research in the study of the Hopi migration between the year 1200 and the late 1300's.

## Tsu'Vo Loop

In the Hopi language Tsu'Vo means "path of the rattlesnake." Here you will find Anasazi petroglpyhs said to be the oldest in the park.

Tsu'Vo Loop is easily accessible to the public.

Stop by the visitor's center to pick up a detailed guide.

# Homolovi Ruins

This site has several well-preserved panels. Near the top of the hill, you will find some ruins that overlook the Little Colorado River.

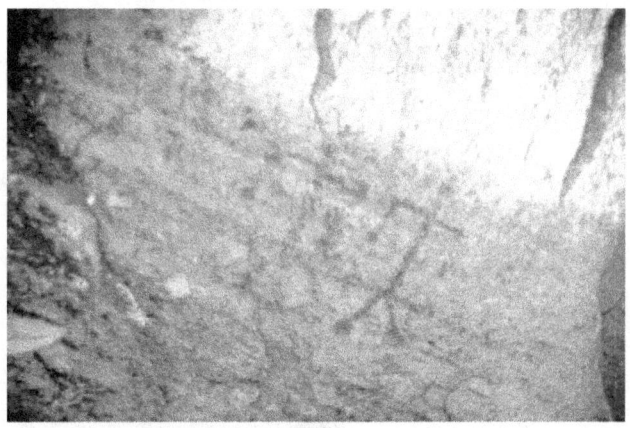

*This is considered one of the oldest sites in the park.*

## Homolovi Kokopelli

Kokopelli's are found all over the Southwest. In Native American stories, the Kokopelli can be understood as a fertility symbol, and is often depicted as a phallic character carrying a pouch of seeds or wearing antlers. In most cases, it also is a request for a fruitful harvest. Kokopelli is a Hopi word roughly meaning "wooden-backed."

*Kokopelli, the flute player.*

# Homolovi Ruins Map

Homolovi Ruins State Park is located approximately 3 miles northeast of Winslow. From Flagstaff, drive east on Interstate 40 to Exit 257, then drive 1.3 miles north on Hwy 87.

Homolovi is open year round except Christmas Day. Accommodations include picnic tables, electric hookups, restrooms, and a dump station.

**Contact:**
Homolovi Ruins State Park
HCR 63, Box 5
Winslow, AZ 86047
Phone: 928-289-4106

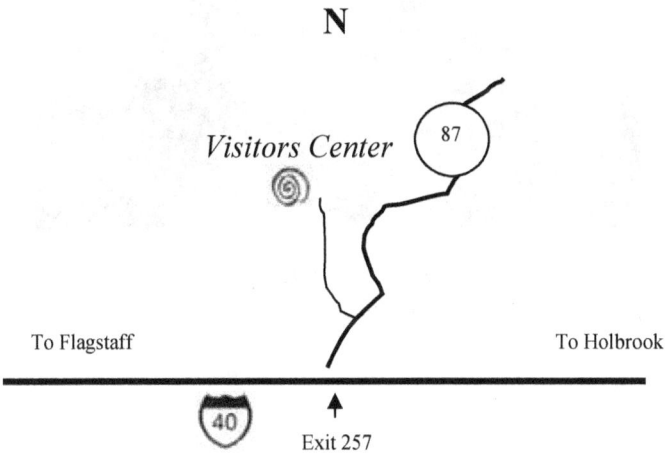

## Inscription Rock

Inscription Rock at Davis Camp is located on the right hand side as you enter the park. A fence is surrounding the petroglpyhs to keep people from treading on them.

All along the fence are numerous plaques that describe the Native Americans' way of life.

Davis Camp offers camping for RVs and tents. Some campsites are close to the Colorado River. It is no wonder why the Indians loved this area.

This petroglyph site can be viewed from the comforts of your car. Bring binoculars and a zoom lens.

*Mohave petroglyphs;*
*Anthropomorphic figures.*

# Inscription Rock Map

From the junction of Hwy 163 and Hwy 95, turn north and drive ½ mile to the Davis Camp. There is an entrance fee to this site.

**Vehicle:** Two-wheel drive accessible.

**Contact:**
Davis Camp Park
2251 Hwy 68
Bullhead City, AZ 86429
Phone: 877-757-0915

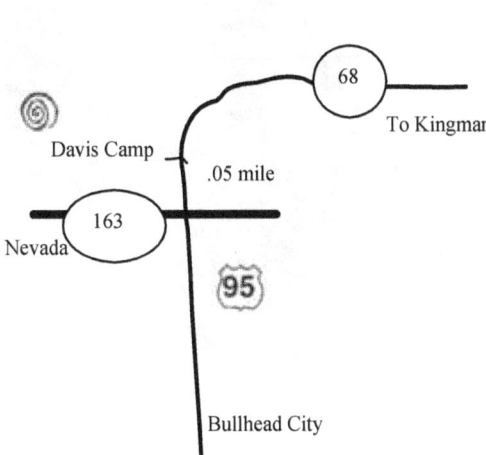

## K5 High Country Adventures

The Little Colorado River flows through the Springerville area. Basalt Cliffs dominate the river and hide some of the more spectacular petroglyphs depicting figures such as elk, deer, cranes, and more. Human-like figures (anthropomorphic) with large hands are found everywhere and were considered a sign of power.

The Anasazi and Mogollon people occupied this area, which probably accounts for the variety of petroglyphs found here. Most of this area is on private property and a guide is highly recommended.

This tour is in a bushwhacking area so be sure to bring a walking stick, long pants, a good pair of hiking boots, and plenty of water.

*Roxanne Knight serves on the Four Corners Heritage Council, pictured next to a petroglyph.*

## K5 High Country Adventures

K5 High County Adventures has access to some of the best rock art to be found anywhere. This is is a fifth- and sixth-generation working ranch. They offer other activities such has horseback riding, fishing, and guided hiking tours.

Register at the Reed's Motel for a guided tour and visit their Indian gallery and bookstore.

**Contact:**
Reed's Lodge
K5 High Country Adventures
514 E. Main
Springerville, AZ 85938
**Phone:** 928-333-4323
**Web Site:** http://www.k5reeds.com/

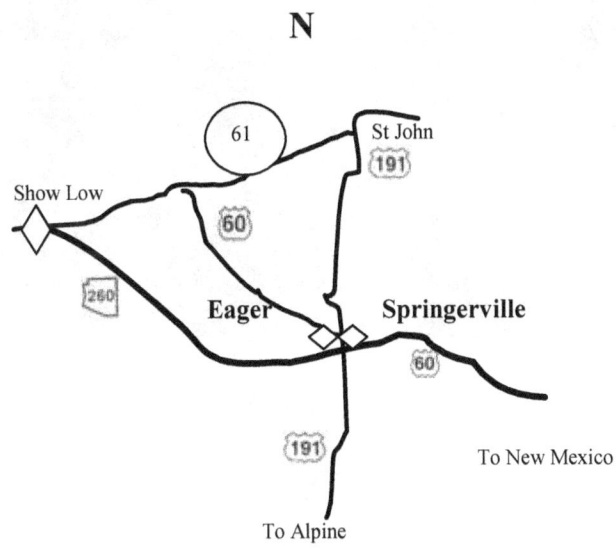

# Katherine Landing

This is a fun-filled place to visit. If you like camping out there are plenty of spaces available. They have a motel, an excellent restaurant, and a small store for all your needs. Katherine Landing also boasts great fishing, and boat rentals are available.

The ranger station will give you a map to a petroglyph site just on the other side of the Colorado River. The petroglyph here is a single boulder that apparently was brought over to this particular area for preservation. Although we do not have much information on this boulder it is in one of our favorite areas to visit. For further information, call 1-800-752-9669

*Relocated boulder.*

## Katherine Landing Map

Katherine Landing is approximately 6 miles from Bullhead City, Ariz., and 30 miles from Kingman. Drive to Country Rt. 68 and follow signs to Katherine Landing. The road is approximately 3.3 miles to the park entrance. An entrance fee is required.

It is well worth staying here if you want to fish, camp, or rent a houseboat.

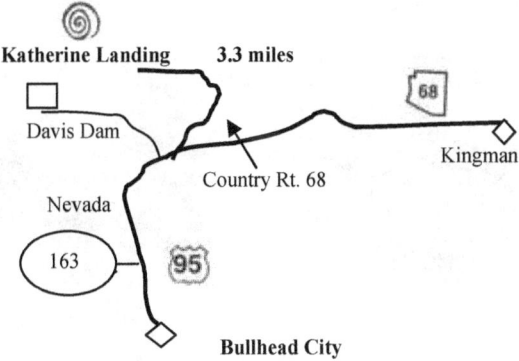

# Keyhole Sink

Just east of Williams is a box canyon known as Keyhole Sink, a watering hole for wild animals. The walls at the sink come alive with rock art. The petroglyphs left by the Cohonina culture, the descendant of the Patayan culture, depict animals (anthropomorphic), hunting scenes, sunbursts, and footprints, just to name a few. At the mouth of the canyon there are interpretive signs that describe Indian life as it was in this area.

We discovered this area and many other prehistoric sites through the Kaibab National Forest District ranger station in Williams.

Williams also has the Grand Canyon Railway Depot Museum as well as a historic train, offering rides to the Grand Canyon.

*One of the petroglyph panels at Keyhole Sink.*

## Keyhole Sink Map

From the town of Williams, head east on I-40 to Exit 171. From Exit 171 drive east on Route 66 for 2 miles to the Oak Hill Snow Play Area. On the right side of the road you will see a parking lot. The trailhead is on the north side of the road. This site is about a 1-mile hike on a well-marked trail. Ask for maps to other areas in Williams at the Williams Forest Service Visitor Center.

**Contact:**
Williams Forest Service Visitor Center
200 W. Railroad Ave.
Williams, AZ 86046
Phone: 928-635-4061

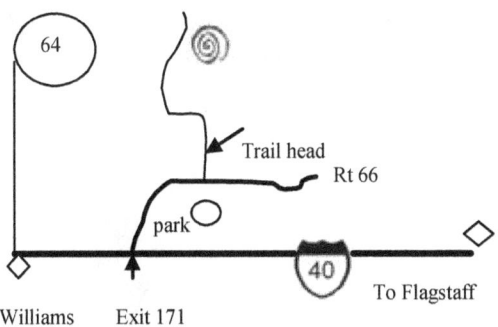

# Kingman Petroglyphs

In 1996, these petroglyphs were added to the National Register of Historical Places. This 2-acre site is owned by Arizona State Land Department's land trust and is open to the public. These petroglyphs are often used to teach local school children the significance of prehistoric rock art.

These petroglyphs seem to have a religious or ceremonial function. What can you see in them?

*Dave Brown next to one of several petroglyphs located in Kingman.*

# Kingman Map

### Northern Avenue Map

This petroglyph site is very easy to get to. From I-40 take Exit 51 and head north on Stockton Hill Road for about 5 miles to Northern Avenue. Turn left onto a dirt road and drive about .3 miles to the first outcrop of black boulders. Rock art can be seen from the parking lot. Binoculars and a zoom lens are suggested.

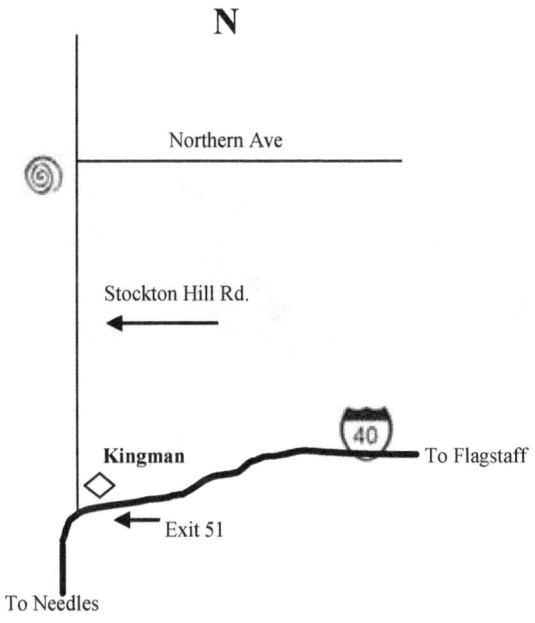

# Kings Canyon Petroglyphs

There is a good map at the beginning of the trail. Follow the wash up a slight grade for about 2 miles of easy walking. The Hohokam petroglyphs are located right in the wash. Look for two human figures that appear to be dancing. A few geometric designs and possibly water signs are very faint and appear to be quite old.

Just above the petroglyphs stands a rock building with some picnic tables for resting or having lunch.

We were there in February and the desert was alive with blooming flowers. A wide-angle lens is best for photographing this particular landscape.

*Petroglyphs in the wash.*

# Kings Canyon Map

As you are heading south on I-10 from Phoenix, you will merge onto 1-19. Take the Ajo Way ramp Exit 99. Turn right off the ramp onto Hwy 86. Drive approximately 5 miles and turn right on Kinney Road, then go 7 more miles to the Desert Museum. There you will pick up the map for Kings Canyon.

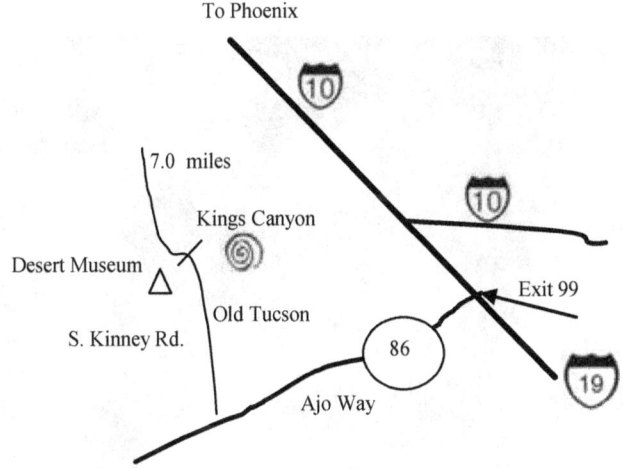

## Kitt Peak National Observatory

Kitt Peak was established in 1957 as the first National Astronomical Observatory. This observatory has the largest collection of telescopes in the world. Visitors can take a free self-guided tour. The observatory also has a national solar observatory exhibit were you can watch scientists operate the largest solar telescope in the world.

A large boulder with petroglyphs was brought to Kitt Peak to preserve it. Hohokam culture made these petroglyphs between 300 A.D. and 1300 A.D. They consist of geometric lines, sheep, deer, and lizards. The King Ranch donated the petroglyph boulder.

*Petroglyph is protected behind a glass case outside.*

# Kitt Peak National Observatory Map

This is a great place for the whole family to explore the same stars and galaxies that prehistoric man observed thousands of years ago.

Head west from Tucson via Route 86 for approximately 50 miles toward Ajo. Pass Three Points Junction and head for S.R. 386 Kitt Peak turnoff. Drive 12 miles to the visitor's center.

**Contact:**
Kitt Peak National Observatory Visitors Center and Museum
Phone: 520-318-8726; call ahead to check dates and hours of operation

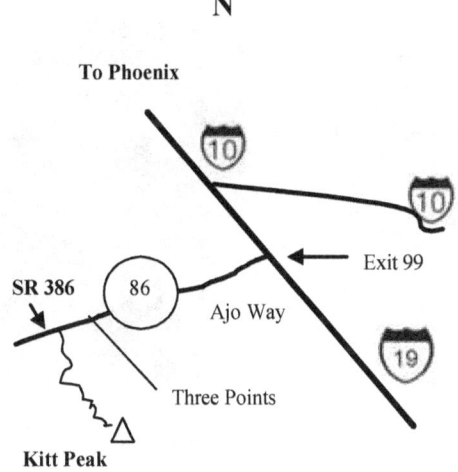

# Lake Havasu City

The London Bridge is the largest antique ever sold. It was brought over here from England and reassembled piece by piece. Beneath the bridge you can catch a ride on the "Starship 2010" of the Blue Water Jet Boat Tours. Take the 2½-hour, 50-mile journey up the Topock Gorge to the Havasu National Wildlife Refuge. The Starship 2010 has a snack bar, large viewing windows, and a climate-controlled cabin.

The tour recounts the history of this part of the Colorado River, and the 3,500-year-old petroglyphs. Bring binoculars and a zoom lens. You just might see a bighorn sheep.

*Petroglyphs overlooking Havasu Lake.*

## Lake Havasu City Map

From Kingman it is approximately 60 miles west on I-40. From Needles, Calif., it is approximately 20 miles east to the Lake Havasu turnoff. Take Exit 9 to Hwy 95. Follow signs to the London Bridge.

**Contact:**
Tour Information
501 English Village
Lake Havasu City, AZ 86403
Phone: 928-855-7171

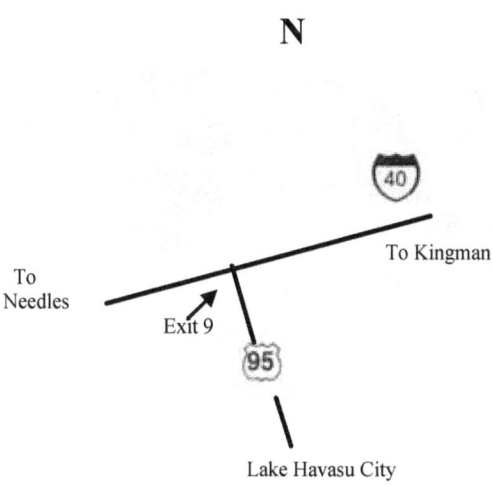

# Lake Mc Hood Park

The best way to reach these petroglyphs is by boat. From the boat launch area head south 2.5 miles through a narrow canyon with some of the most spectacular sandstone cliffs that tower over 200 feet high. The Anasazi petroglyphs are on both sides of the canyon. The first ones you come to are on the left side. Keep an eye out for a sandy beach just big enough to land your boat. The next petroglyphs are located on your right within 100 yards. If you pass the pump house wall you went too far. The petroglyphs consist of sheep and human figures with very elaborate details.

Lake Mc Hood also invites anglers to some great fishing and the public can enjoy swimming and camping just a few minutes from Winslow.

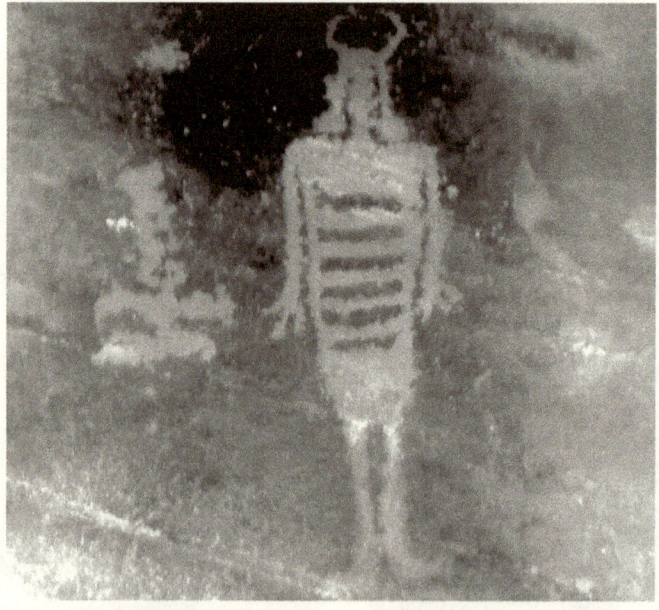

Anthropomorphic figure wearing buffalo headdress.

## Lake Mc Hood Park Map

From I-40 take the Winslow exit (Exit 252) and drive east on the main road. Follow the signs to Hwy 87 and drive south for 2 miles to Mile Marker 341. Turn left to Hwy 99. Drive 4.2 miles on Hwy 99. Mc Hood Park is between M.M. 39 and M.M. 38.

**Vehicles:** two-wheel drive accessible

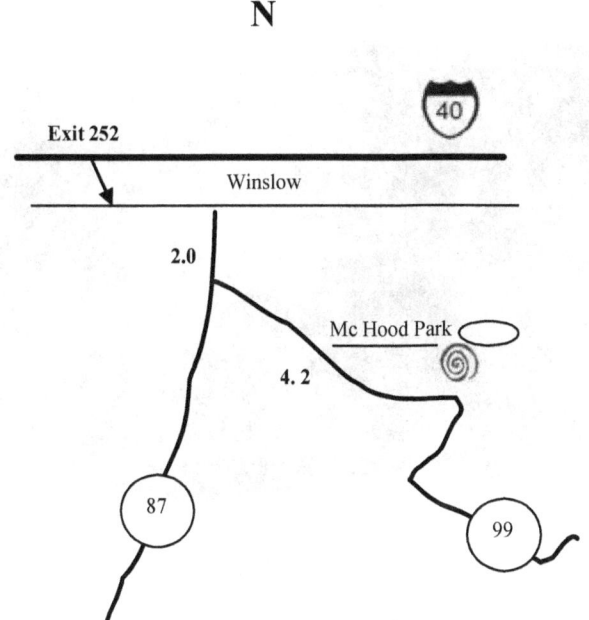

## Las Guijas Petroglyphs

This area was inhabited by the Hohokam culture sometime between 300 B.C. and 1400 A.D. In the 1400's, the Pima and Papago Indians moved into the area and gave this place its name, meaning, "water that comes up."

The rock art is located on the rubble of rock facing east. The petroglyphs consist of concentric circles, star burst, sun, and abstract motifs. This site seems like it represents the study of the motion of stars and planets. Arivaca is a border town and one should remain vigilant while hiking in this area.

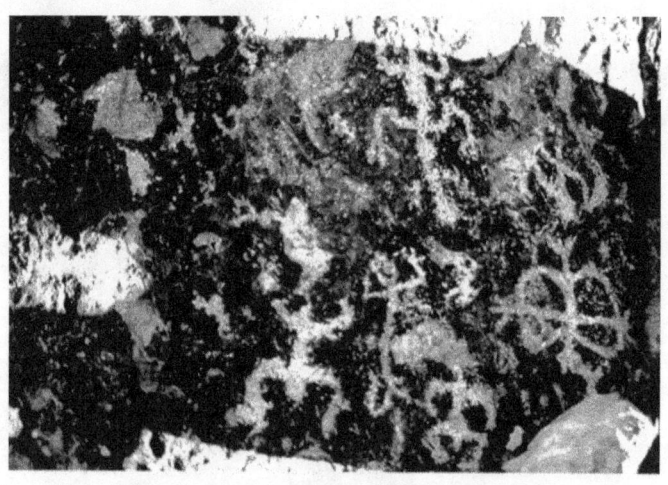

*This boulder depicts lots of lizards.*

## Las Guijas Petroglyph Map

From the town of Arivaca, head northeast on Arivaca Road to Mile Marker 6 and 7. Turn left onto a dirt road and drive about 5 miles north. On the right there is an old mill site foundation. Park and head north through the dry wash; the rubble of rocks is facing east. This area is called Las Guijas and is on Bureau of Land Management property.

(Refer to page 8 under "Laws")

**Vehicle:** Four-wheel drive recommended

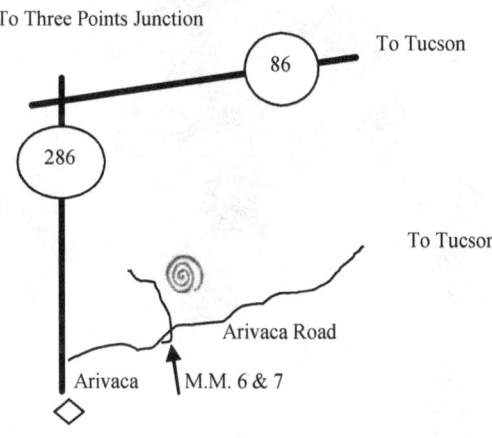

## Laws Springs

Laws Springs was named after a fellow that traveled with the Beal Expedition in 1857-59. They surveyed for one of the first wagon roads west. Beal was the one who brought camels on his expedition. The camels later were let loose to run amuck throughout the desert. Arizona passed a law prohibiting the hunting of camels, and it's still on the books today.

The petroglyphs are a short walk from the parking area. The rock art contains historic and prehistoric messages. The springs supported life here for hundreds of years. There is a monument at the springs that explains the history. This is a very unique place to spend the day.

*Petroglpyhs left by Cohonina culture.*

## Law Springs Map

From Williams, go east on Route 66 to Highway 64. Drive north 5 miles to Spring Valley Road, Frontage Road 141. Turn right and continue for about 7 miles, then turn left on F.R. 730 and drive 3 more miles. Turn left on F.R. 115 for about 1½ miles to F.R. 203.

Follow the sign to the parking area. The trails are well marked and it is an easy walk about ¼ mile from the parking lot. Bring a lunch and spend the day.

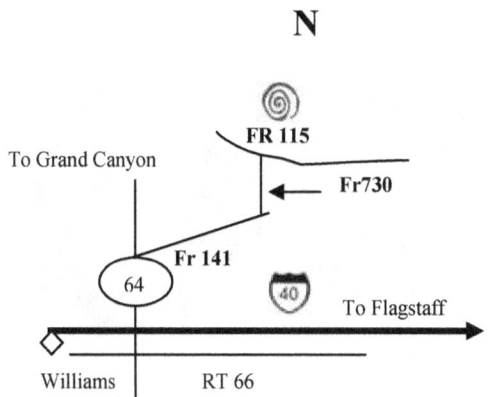

## Little Black Mountain

Little Black Mountain… what a name! This mountain is about as red as it gets. So off we go looking for a black mountain with more than 500 glyphs.

These petroglyphs represent multiple cultures from the Great Basin to Western Anasazi and the Lower Colorado River.

Some of the rock art in this area features zoomorphic animals such as turtles, sheep, and bear paws. The sheep are spectacular, and were probably left by the Virgin River Puebloan culture (1050 A.D. to 1150 A.D.).

This is a very easy trail to walk. Early morning or afternoon is best for photographing these petroglyphs.

*Sheep at Little Black Mountain.*

# Little Black Mountain Map

It is best to go to the Bureau of Land Management to pick up a map to this site.

**Contact:**
BLM Office
345 E. Riverside Drive
St. George, UT 84790
Phone: 435-688-3200
Fax: 435-688-3258

From the Arizona state line, drive north and take Exit 6 on Hwy 15. As soon as you are off the ramp turn right on Bluff Road and follow it around till you find Riverside Road. The Bureau of Land Management's office is on the left side.

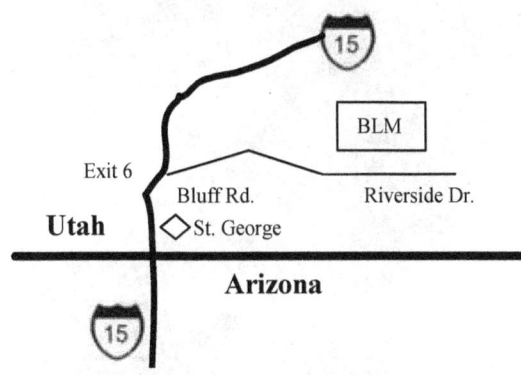

# Lyman Lake State Park

Lyman Lake State Park has an extensive display of rock art that dates from 8000 B.C. To 1598 A.D. Several cultures are represented in this area, the Archaic being the oldest.

There are two sites located in the park. A boat is needed for the one located on the east side of the lake; the site near the campground is a self-guided tour.

There are two prehistoric pueblos, which have been excavated by archaeologists. The park office can arrange a tour of these pueblos.

This park is one of the finest state parks in Arizona. Lots of RV spaces are available or you can rent a yurt or small cabin.

*Cougar and eagle.*

# Lyman Lake Map

From Holbrook, drive southeast on Hwy 180 to the town of St. Johns. Proceed approximately 13 miles south toward Springerville on Hwy 191. Lyman Lake is on the east side of the highway, or 19 miles north of Springerville.

**Vehicle:** Two-wheel drive accessible

For more information, contact Lyman Lake State Park at 928-337-4441.

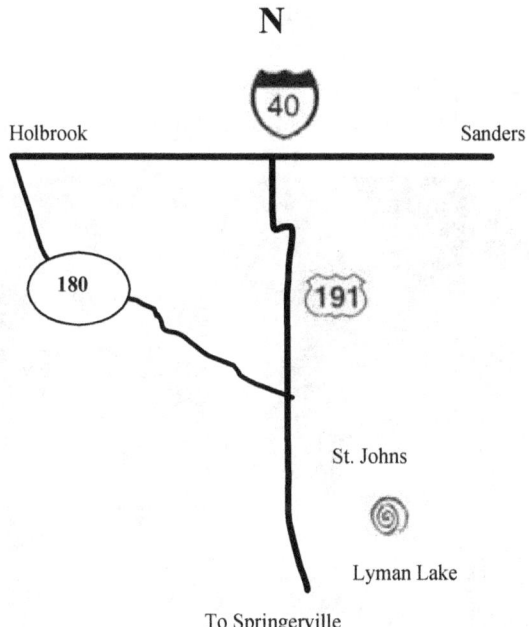

## Martinez Lake

Martinez Lake is a little oasis in the desert with some really nice petroglyphs that can be seen by boat. The Patayan culture inhabited this area and left these petroglyphs here some 500 years ago. The petroglyphs are on Martinez Lake, which is a tributary of the Colorado River. These petroglyphs are only accessible by boat. We signed on for a jet boat ride at the general store down by the docks.

The tour lasts most of the day. We saw bighorn sheep, great blue herons, and ducks of every kind. We stopped to photograph some petroglyphs located on the bank of the river. A zoom lens definitely helps here. This trip is worth the time and money, so load up the whole family and enjoy the tour and the lunch served at an old ghost town.

*Petroglyph found along the river.*

# Martinez Lake Map

From Yuma, drive 25 miles north on U.S. 95 and turn west on Martinez Lake Road. Drive 10.5 miles to Mile Marker 46. Turn right at the Imperial sign and drive 2 miles. From here you can go to the visitors center or follow signs to Fishers Landing. They have an R.V. park, boat docks, bar, restaurant, and a great place to fish.

**For reservations contact:**
Yuma River Tours
1920 Arizona Ave.
Yuma, AZ
Phone: 928-783-4400

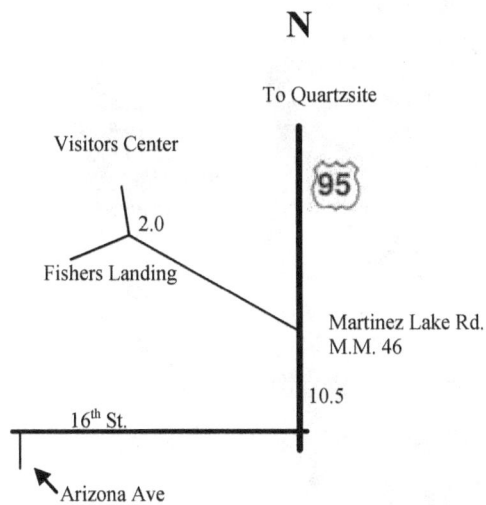

## Millville Petroglyphs

Just south of Tombstone is the mining town of Millville. Millville was established around the 1870's along the San Pedro River. A fancy town in its time, Millville was in the business of processing silver ore.

The Bureau of Land Management (BLM) has constructed the "Petroglyph Discovery Trail" with self-guided tour markers to lead the way. The roundtrip is an easy to moderate 2.5-mile hike. Some of the glyphs are up about 25 to 30 feet from the ground floor. A camera with a zoom lens will help capture the best shots. These petroglyphs are from the Hohokam culture and are said to be 600 years old.

*One of many boulders found at site.*

# Millville Map

From the town of Tombstone, head south on Charleston Road for approximately 9 miles. Turn right just past the power lines. You can also park at the San Pedro River Park another 1 mile down the road and walk or drive back. Discovery Trail is on the northwest side of the road.

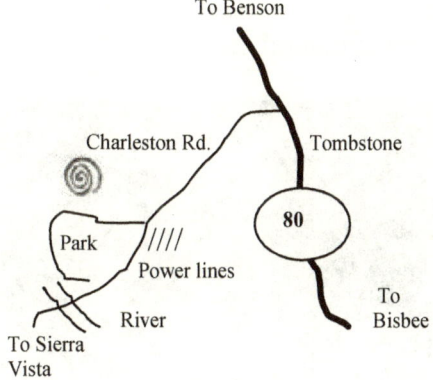

# Moenkopi Petroglyphs

Moenkopi is located on the Navajo reservation just southwest of Tuba City. Moenkopi is known for its dinosaur tracks. The best way to see these tracks is by Navajo guide. A donation for their time and expertise is expected.

Up the road from the dinosaur tracks is Willow Creek Canyon. More than 100 petroglyphs can be found here. The detailed petroglyphs are said to be done by the Hopi and Navajo. The artists were very skilled and detailed in their work. This seems to be a ceremonial area with a lot of spiritual energy. A tour here will probably cost a few bucks but it's worth it. Don't forget you are taking a tour by the Navajo—not Hopi. It might cost you more for the tour if you make that mistake.

*Some of the detailed petroglyphs located at Willow Creek.*

# Moenkopi Petroglyphs Map

From the town of Flagstaff, drive north on Hwy 89 for approximately 75 miles. Turn right on Hwy 160 and drive 5 miles heading toward Tuba City. The dinosaur tracks are on the north side; watch for large directional signs.

N

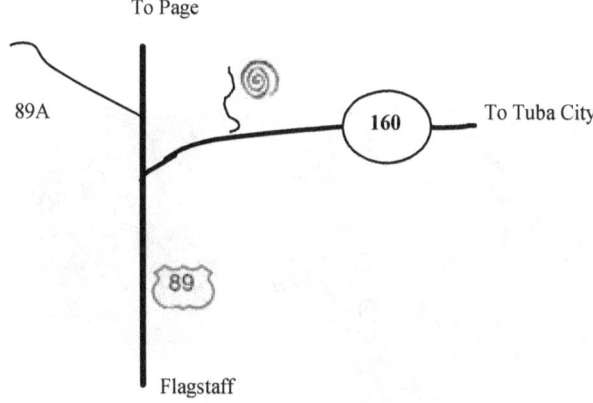

## Monument Valley Petroglyphs "Mystery Valley"

Sign up at Gouldings Lodge for a trip with a Navajo guide to see places you'll never forget. The tour consist of a visit to John Ford's movie locations, where some of the best Westerns were made, followed by a visit to the Anasazi ruins. Look for a detailed petroglyph of a large sheep jumping over a smaller one. Mystery Valley also has pictographs that date back some 600 years. Numerous handprints and human figures adorn the walls.

You will need a camera with a wide-angle lens to capture the beautiful views and the 1,000-ft. monoliths.

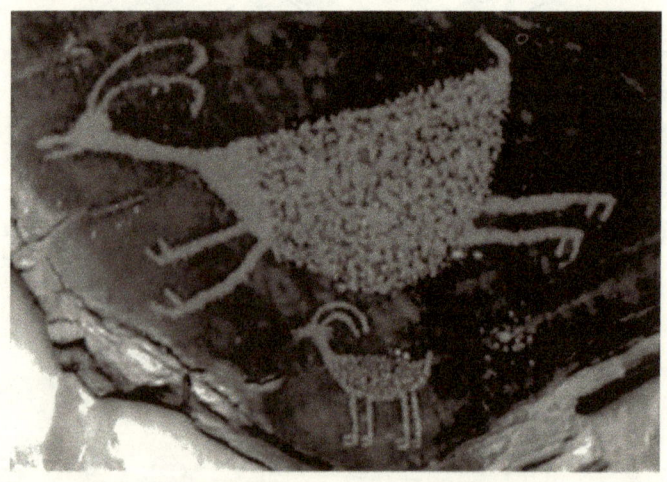

*Large sheep jumping over little one.*

# Monument Valley Map

Monument Valley is located in the northern part of Arizona on the Arizona/Utah border. It is Approximately 24 miles from the town of Kayenta.

**Vehicles:** Two-wheel drive accessible.

**Contact:**
Gouldings Trading Post
P.O. Box 360001
1000 Main St.
Monument Valley, UT 84536
Phone:   435-727-3231
Web site: www.gouldings.com

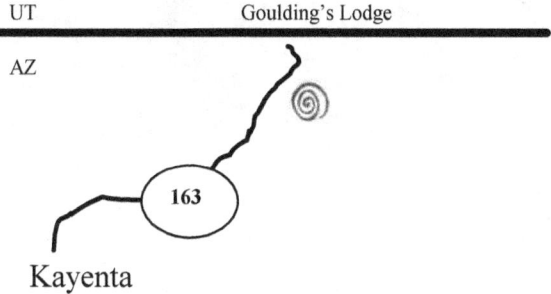

# Nampaweap

Nampaweap is located in Billy Goat Canyon along the Arizona Strip. Nampaweap means "foot canyon," a name given by the Paiute Indians. The nearest town is 70 miles away via dirt road. Plan on spending the whole day here.

Before you get to this site, you may want to stop at Trumbull School House, an old one-room school.

Once you arrive at the Nampaweap site an interpretative sign leads you to the petroglyphs. It is an easy ¼-mile trek and there are no facilities.

The Archaic, Anasazi, and Paiute etched distinctive symbols throughout the canyon walls. This may have been a trail used to travel to the Grand Canyon.

**Please be aware of your footing in this area. It is a long way back to town.**

*This looks territorial?*

## Nampaweap Map

Nampaweap is located along the Arizona Strip and it is approximately 70 miles from St. George, Utah, to the site. The Bureau of Land Management will provide a map to this location.

**Vehicle:** Two-wheel drive accessible, weather permitting.

**Contact:**
Bureau of Land Management
Arizona Strip Field Office
345 E. Riverside Drive
St. George, UT 84790-6714
Phone: 435-688-3200
Fax: 435-688-3258

**(Refer to the map located on page 95)**

# Organ Pipe Cactus

Organ Pipe Cactus National Monument is located in southern Arizona along the Mexican border. Crowley Canyon contains thousands of spectacular petroglyphs but has been temporarily closed to the public due to border problems. There is talk of possibly opening this area soon.

Organ Pipe is like no other place on earth. Several trails offer a great opportunity to view the unique desert beauty of this very special area

The best time to visit is October through April. Plan on enjoying the narrated guided walks and taking advantage of the camping and picnicking.

*Petroglyph found at the visitors center possibly left by the Patayan culture.*

## Organ Pipe Cactus Map

From Ajo, drive south 12 miles to Why. From Why drive another 20 miles to Mile Marker 75. This is the entrance to Organ Pipe Cactus National Monument.

**Vehicle**: Two-wheel drive accessible.

**Contact:**
Organ Pipe Cactus National Monument
10 Organ Pipe Drive
Ajo, AZ 85321
Phone: 520-387-6849

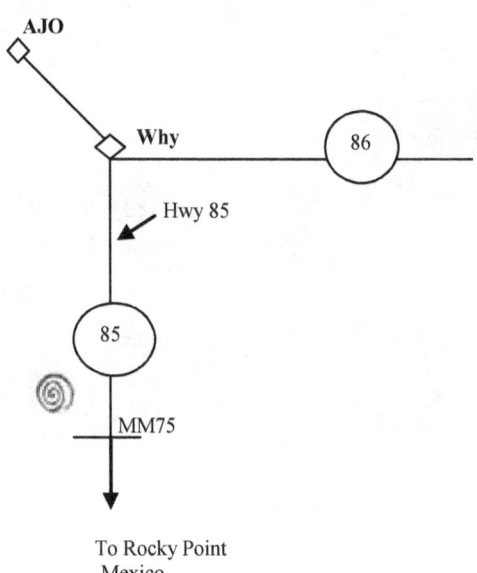

## Painted Rock

There are over 700 petroglyphs at Painted Rock. One of the most impressive petroglyphs has a calendar with a human figure and sunburst carved on it. During the winter solstice, on December 21$^{st}$, the sun shines directly on the center of the sunburst.

This is the only time of the year this happens.

These engraved figures are attributed to the Hohokam Indians, who vanished as a definable group during the mid 1400's.

The explorer Juan Bautista de Anza, who possibly left his mark on these rocks, traveled here on his way to California in 1775. These huge boulders served as a landmark for travelers following the old Gila Trail.

*Myrna Bicknell & Leonard B. Secklin at Painted Rock.*

# Painted Rock Map

Painted Rock petroglyphs are located just west of Gila Bend. Take I-8 west 15 miles to Painted Rock Road (Exit 102). Drive north approximately 10 miles. The petroglyphs are located at Painted Rock Campground. There are picnic tables and toilets and the road is accessible for all RVs.

A small fee may be required.

**Contact:**
BLM
Phoenix Field Office
21605 N. 7th Ave.
Phoenix, AZ 85027
Phone: 623-580-5500

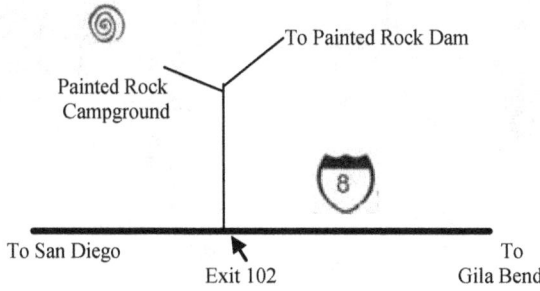

# Palatki Ruins Petroglyphs

It is nice to visit a rock art site that has petroglyphs and pictographs in the same area. This site is said to be about 6,000 years old. The pictographs have a variety of colors. Red pigment was made from several forms of minerals such as iron oxide, red ochre, and cinnabar. The black comes from charcoal carbon and manganese oxide. The white was created from gypsum, talc, and limestone. The pigments were crushed with a mortar and pestle then mixed with a binder. A brush made from hair was probably used to paint the surface of the rock.

Some of the styles of these red pictographs can also be found throughout Utah's Barrier Canyon. I recommend stopping at Palatki visitors center before you visit the ruins.

*Sinagua shield pictograph.*

## Palatki Ruins Map

From Sedona, take 89A south just past Mile Marker 365 (look for a group of mailboxes). Turn right (north) onto a dirt road F.R. 525 and drive about 5 miles where the road turns into F.R. 795. Drive another 3 ½ miles and arrive at Palatki Ruins.

**Vehicle:** Two-wheel drive, weather permitting.
**Contact:**
Palatki Ruins Visitor Center
Red Rock Ranger District
P.O. Box 20429, Sedona AZ 86341 Phone: 928-282-4119
Web site:
www.redrockcountry.org/recreation/cultural/v-bar-v.shtml

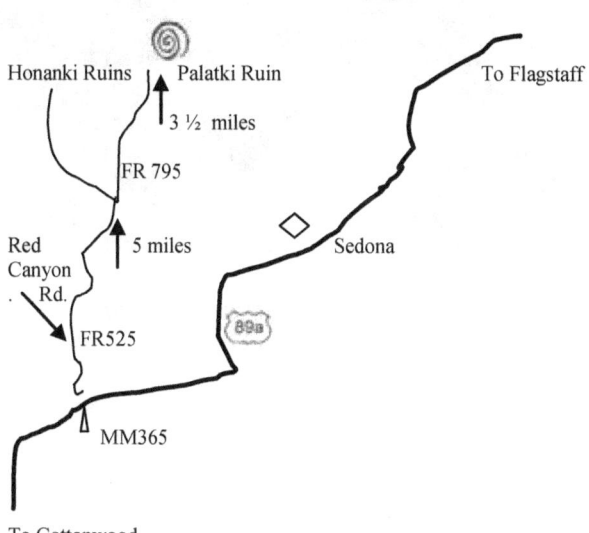

# Partridge Creek Petroglyphs

The petroglyphs at Partridge Creek are Archaic, which puts them right up there with some of the oldest petroglyphs in North America, ranging from 4,000 to 6,000 years old. One of the largest sites in all of Northern Arizona, this area is often featured in rock art lectures highlighting the age and density of this collection, estimated to be 600 to 800 pieces.

In 2006, Dr. Karen Peters and her husband Ron Peters won the Governor's Award for historic preservation in the private sector. They are currently working with the Sharlot Hall Museum and Yavapai Community College to properly record and document this site.

*Eric Gorham in front of petroglyphs.*

# Partridge Creek Petroglyphs Map

Partridge Creek is located near the town of Ash Fork. To visit this area you will need to make reservations first with either Dr. Karen Peters or Ron Peters. The Peters will give you a guided tour and share the information that the Yavapai and Hopi people have shared with them.

**Vehicle:** Two-wheel drive recommended, weather permitting.

**Contact:**
The Petroglyphs at Partridge Creek
P.O. Box 1065
Ash Fork, AZ 86320
Phone: 928-925-6475

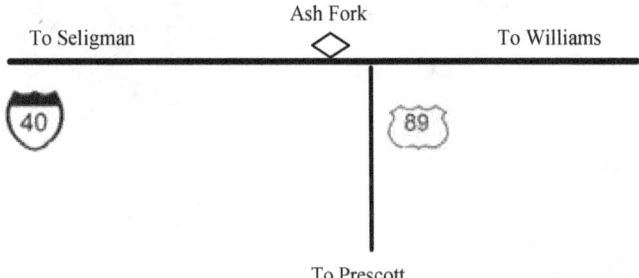

## Patagonia Lake Petroglyph

With 740 acres of trails and a lake that is 2.5 miles long, Patagonia Lake State Park is a place where you will want to spend a few days. The park has camping, fishing, a marina, and a store. They also have restrooms, showers, and a dump station for R.V.s

One of the things I found interesting was the bird watching. Patagonia Lake State Park is home to more than 200 species of birds. Enjoy "Introduction to Birding," just one of the many programs and activities found at this park.

The rock art is located on the other side of the lake and is somewhat difficult to find; a boat is the way to go here. Take your time to enjoy it all. Find the petroglyph shown below and get some good pictures of those rare feathered inhabitants.

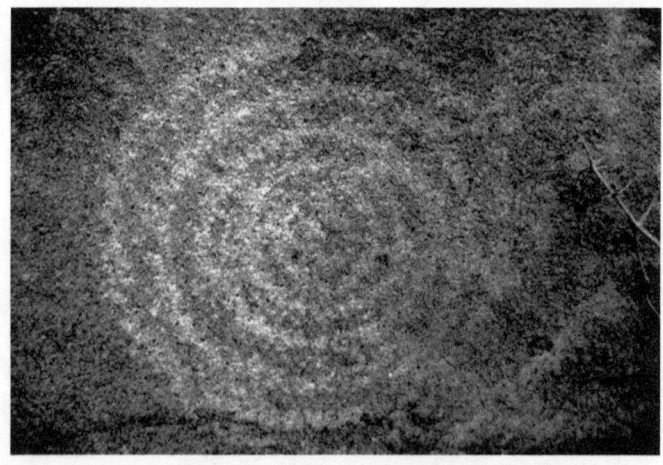

*Concentric circle hidden behind a large boulder at park.*

# Patagonia Lake Map

From I-10 Tucson, drive east to Hwy 83, south to Hwy 82. From the junction of Hwy 83 and Hwy 82 drive west 7 miles past the town of Patagonia.

Visit the town of Patagonia; it is a great little town with a lot of history.

**Vehicle:** Two-wheel drive recommended.
**Contact:**
Patagonia Lake State Park
400 Patagonia Lake Road
Patagonia, AZ 85624

**Phone:** 520-287-6965

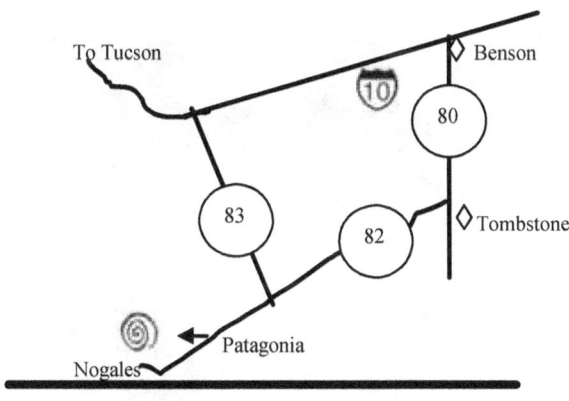

## Petrified Forest

About 225 million years ago, Petrified Forest National Park was underwater. The mineral-rich water exchanged silica and quartz with the organic matter of the trees, which created some of the most beautiful petrified redwoods (rock) in the world.

Petrified Forest National Park has hundreds of petroglyphs and pictographs left behind by the prehistoric Puebloans.

Puerco Ruins, which dates back to about 1200-1350 A.D., is open for public tours. One of the more interesting sites is Newspaper Rock. It is unique in having hundreds of petroglyphs located on one large rock face. Binoculars or a telescope are needed to view this site.

The 27-mile drive through the park is well worth taking. There are eight different overlooks along this road with great views of the Painted Desert.

*Cougar.*

## Petrified Forest Map

From Holbrook, drive east on I-40 to Petrified Forest National Park. Turn off at Exit 311 and follow the signs to the visitors center. The park is open all year round. There is no camping in the park; it is open for day use only. There is an admission charge. For more information, contact the park at 928-524-6228.

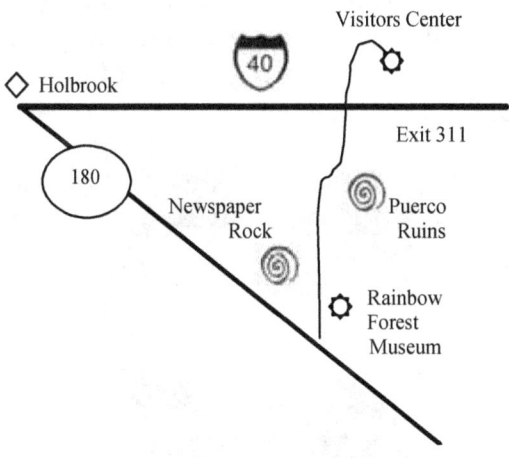

# Phantom Ranch

There is something majestic about the Grand Canyon, which is like no other place on earth. Not only can you see it; you can also feel it. Some people think that rock art has spiritual powers and if one draws from that power, one may find some help along the way. The rock art documents spiritual and special events telling us stories of the past. Several cultures inhabited this area such as the Archaic and Cohonina.

Bright Angels Trail takes us to some of these places on our way to the Phantom Ranch. The ranch was built in 1922 out of wood and native stone in a picturesque surrounding, making this a special place to visit.

Whether you travel to Phantom Ranch by foot, mule, or raft, the spiritual powers of this place will help you understand the importance of preserving this for future generations.

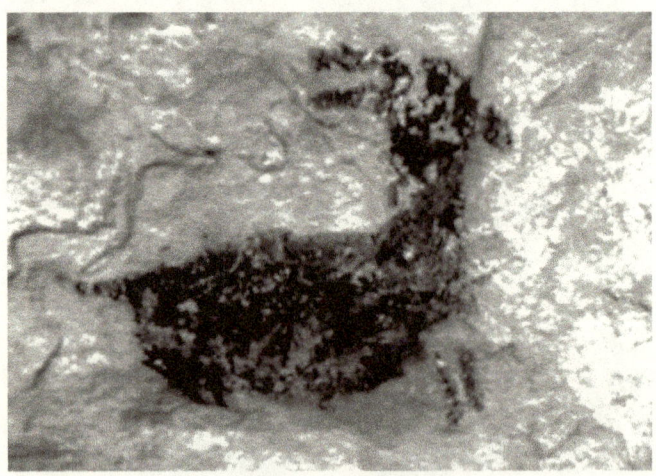

*Pictograph of sheep.*

# Phantom Ranch Map

From the town of William, drive north 55 miles on Hwy 64 to the entrance of the Grand Canyon. The ranger will provide a map of the park and special directions to the Phantom Ranch.

**Contact:**
Xanterra Parks & Resorts
Central Reservations
6312 South Fiddlers Green Circle, Suite 600N
Greenwood Village, CO 80111
Phone: Toll-free within the U.S.: 888-29-PARKS (888.297.2757)
 E-mail: reserve-gcsr@xanterra.com
For same-day reservations or to reach a lodge guest, call 928-638-2631.
Web site:
**www.grandcanyonlodges.com/phantom-ranch-427.html**

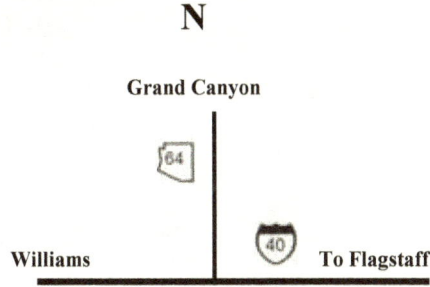

# Picture Rocks Retreat

Picture Rocks Retreat is private property and permission from the office is required to visit.

The Hohokam petroglyphs are a short walk from the two parking lots. The glyphs are located in a dry wash on a boulder about 30 feet off the ground. A zoom lens and binoculars are most suited for locating these magical works of art.

The hunting scene and the dancing humans holding hands are my favorite. There are two-headed animals and many geometric designs. The trail also leads to a desert cactus garden with every kind of cactus found in Arizona. Take the time to visit this very peaceful area.

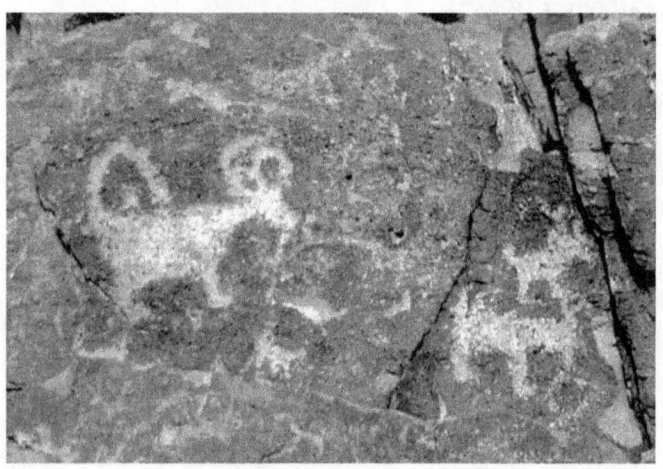

*Bighorn sheep.*

## Picture Rocks Retreat Map

From Tucson, take 1-10 west to Exit 248 (Ina Road). Drive south about 4 miles to Wade Road. Wade Road will turn into Picture Rock Road. Continue approximately 6 miles to Picture Rock Retreat, located on the right-hand side.

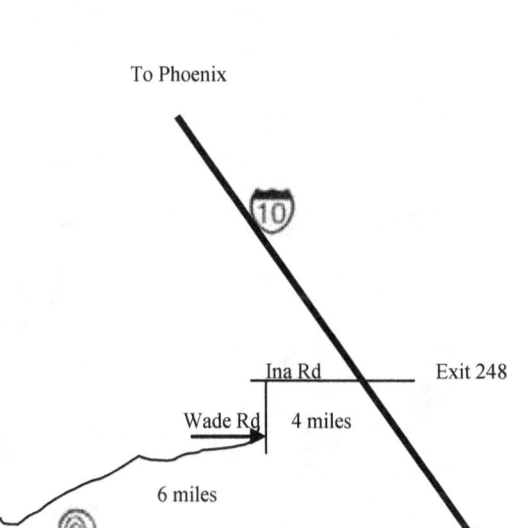

## Polimana Pictographs

Black Canyon Auto Tour starts at the Chevelon Heber Ranger Stations where you can pick up a brochure for a self-guided tour to some of Arizona's most exciting history.

Outlaws and desperados were part of the Pleasant Valley Feud. Cattlemen and sheepherders fought over fertile grasslands. General Crook's Trail passed this way during the Apache wars.

This self-guided tour takes you to some beautiful red pictographs that were painted on a rock by the Mogollon Culture some 1,000 years ago. Just down the road, visit a cave shelter that dates back 900 years or more. Look up at the cave ceiling and see a large orange lizard. This trip has eight stops along the way and takes most of the day.

**This is some of Arizona's best kept history. Enjoy.**

*Note far-right figure.*
*Could these be Atlatl spears?*

# Polimana Pictographs Map

Bring zoom lenses and binoculars for best viewing.

The ranger station is located in the town of Overgaard and the pictographs are just down the road in Heber.

**Vehicle:** Two-wheel drive accessible, weather permitting.

**Contact:**
Chevelon-Heber Ranger District
P.O. Box 968
Overgaard, AZ 85933
Phone: 520-535-4481

## Prescott Lakes

We were told about this petroglyph site from locals who live in Prescott. Petroglyphs in a housing tract sounds interesting so we loaded up our station wagon and headed out to the site. We found an array of rock art from the Anasazi, Hohokam, and Sinagua cultures that took several hours to see. I was really impressed with the way they were displayed in this beautiful subdivision.

The sidewalk led to four park sites. Each park site has a plaque describing the meaning of the petroglyphs. This is one of the best rock art learning experiences one can have.

*Geometric design.*

# Prescott Lakes
*(PARK ONE)*

This is the first plaque that you will encounter. It displays 10 of the petroglyphs in this area.

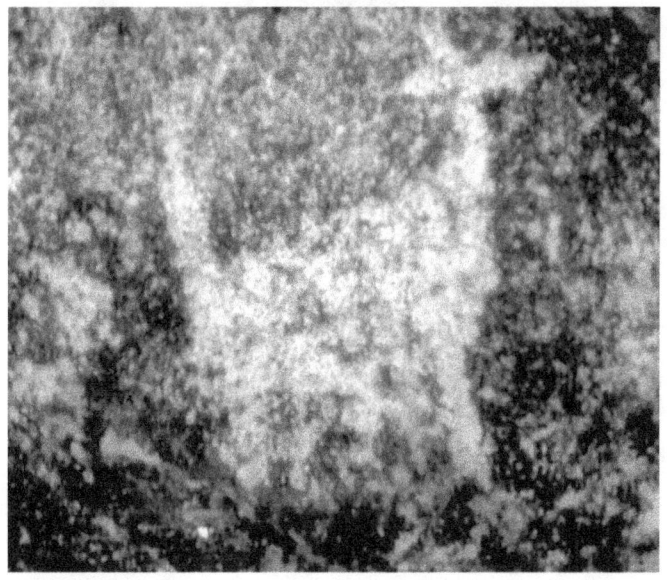

*This park is located at Golden Bear and E. Smoke Tree Lane intersection. No. 9 is Mountain Lion.*

# Prescott Lakes
*(PARK TWO)*

This is the second plaque that displays
10 more petroglyphs.

*This site is located at Thoroughbred and E. Smoke Tree Lane. This petroglyph is No. 4 on the panel, possibly representing a sheep dancing or running*

# Prescott Lakes
*(PARK THREE)*

*Park Three is located at the lake with the waterfall. This petroglyph is No. 3, and depicts a horned toad.*

# Prescott Lakes
*(PARK FOUR)*

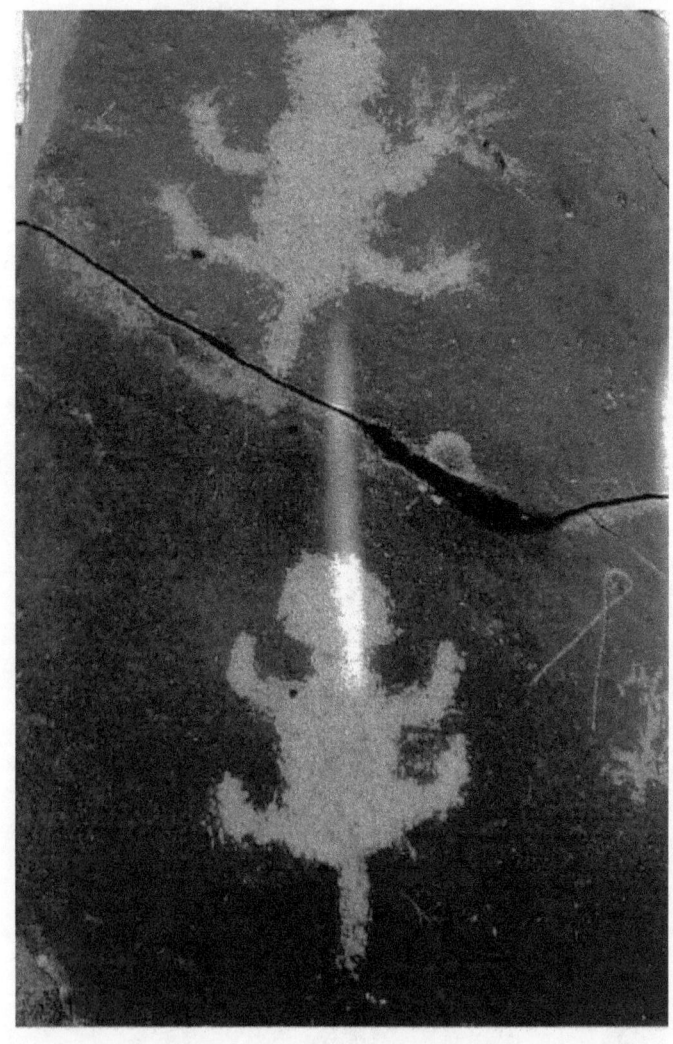

*This is a lizard or a frog.*
*Park Four is located at Durham Drive.*

# Prescott Lakes Map

Prescott Lakes is easy to find. At the junction of Prescott Lakes Highway and Hwy 89, you will see a large waterfall. Turn toward the waterfall and drive up the hill about ½ mile. Turn left onto Smoke Tree Drive. The petroglyphs are on the left side of the road.

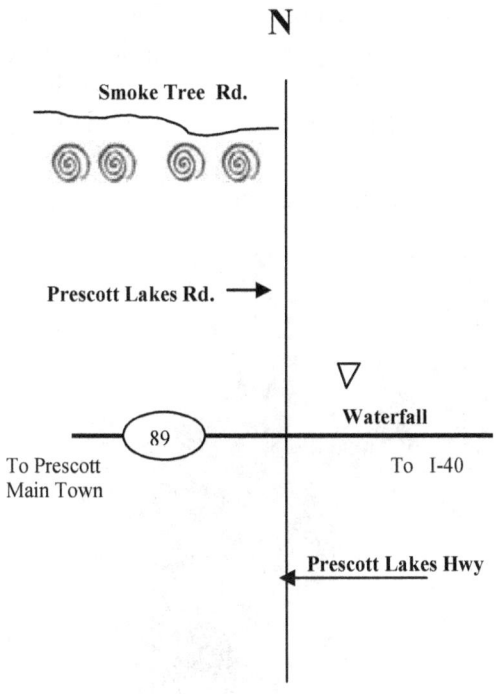

## Robson's Mining World

When I first heard about Robson's Mining Town, I imagined a town with crumbling buildings, litter, and broken bottles. In reality, Robson has the world's largest collection of antique mining equipment. There are more than thirty buildings that are still standing and are full of antiques and artifacts.

I came to see the Indian artifacts and petroglyphs. This rock art site is about three miles round trip from the main street in Robson. We found only two boulders with petroglyphs under a large saguaro cactus in the Black Tanks area. The rock art is for the most part geometric designs. Plan on spending the whole day at Robson's Town as they have something for everyone, including a great lunch.

*Boulder located near saguaro cactus.*

## Robson's Mining World Map

A map with directions to the petroglyphs is available at the store in Robson. The hike to the petroglyphs is fairly easy. But when you reach the canyon, you will have to do some boulder hopping. It is a "snaky-looking" area so watch your step! A bed & breakfast is available in town.

## CLOSED DOWN

Robson's Mining World
P.O. Box 3465
Wickenburg, AZ 85358
Phone: 928-685-2609
Web site: www.robsonsminingworld.com

**Directions:** From Wickenburg drive west on Hwy 60 for 24 miles. Turn right or north for 4 miles and between Mile Marker 89 and 90 turn left onto Robson's Mining World.

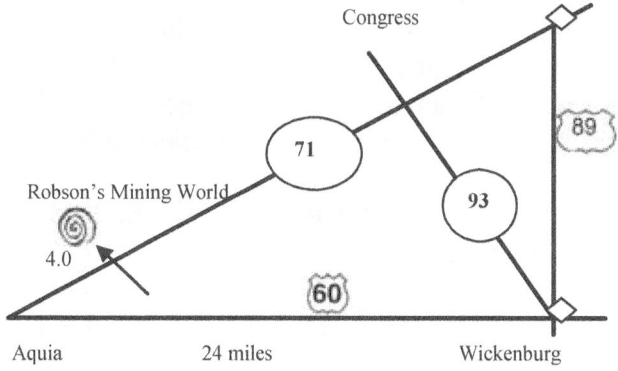

## Rock Art Canyon Ranch

This oasis is a must-see. It has probably one of the finest collections of petroglyphs in the entire Southwest. Archaeologists believe these petroglyphs were etched into the walls of the Chevelon Canyon some 4,000 years ago

The last remaining bunkhouse of the Hashknife Outfit (The Aztec Land and Cattle Co.) stands in full restoration at Rock Art Canyon Ranch. During the 1800's this two-million-acre ranch was the largest ranching operation in Arizona.

Today, the ranch extends its hospitality by offering a large dining hall and a pioneer cowboy museum with hundreds of artifacts of Western life as well as those of the Anasazi culture. This is where the U.S. Cavalry stayed just before going into the last Apache battle. The battle site can be visited today.

The ranch includes family-style entertainment and dining, storytelling, group sing-alongs and breathtaking sunsets.

Rock Art Canyon Ranch is perfect for reunions, scout groups, weddings, or just about any social function. This ranch is a piece of Arizona history and should be on the top of your list of things to do. Reservations are required.

**For further information call 928-288-3260.**

# Rock Art Canyon Ranch Petroglyph

*One of many human-like figures found at
Rock Art Canyon Ranch.*

## Saguaro National Park

Trails lead to two different petroglyph sites at Signal Hill in Saguaro National Park West.

Several rock art styles are represented in this area from the Archaic culture to the Hohokam cultures. The first site has a few pinwheels laid out on a boulder. The second has a large spiral. Spirals may represent migration. The same symbol is used today to represent our galaxy.

Books, maps and trail guides are for sale at the visitor's center. Campgrounds are available throughout the park.

*Saguaro petroglyph overlooks the valley.*

## Saguaro National Park Map

From Tucson, head north on I-10 to Exit 248 (Ina Road). Drive west approximately 4 miles to Wade Road, which becomes Picture Rocks Road. Drive 4 miles farther to Golden Gate Road. Turn left. This road will take you to Signal Hill Trail.

**Contact:**
Saguaro National Park
3693 S. Old Spanish Trail
Tucson, AZ 85730
Phone: 520-733-5100

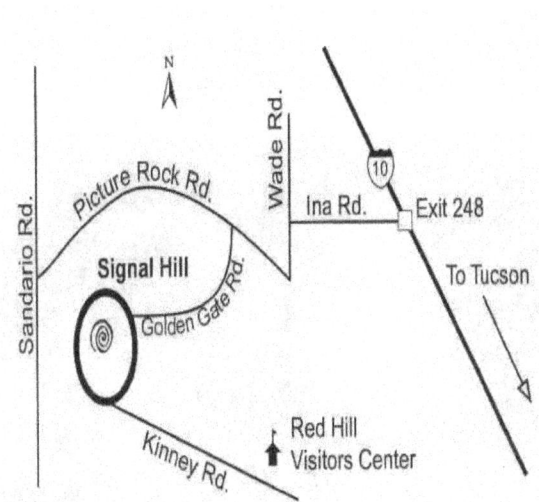

# Sears Point

Sears Point is one of the best rock art sites in southwestern Arizona. The petroglyph panels dominate the large boulder outcrops with a variety of zoomorphic (animal) figures, such as elk, deer, sheep, cougar, and lizards to name a few. The Hohokam culture inhabited this area between 300 A.D. to 1300 A.D. The Bureau of Land Management has estimated that there are several thousand petroglyphs within this one area. There are historic names carved into the rocks dating back to the 1840's when trappers and the gold rush groups passed through.

Sears Point rock art site is precious, like all similar places, and must be preserved for future generations. Bring a wide-angle lens and a tripod for an unbelievable photo op.

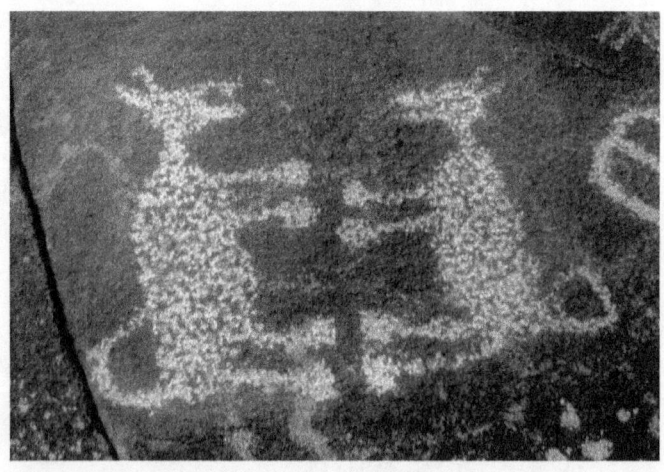

*Are they talking?*

## Sears Point Map

From Gila Bend, head west 39 miles on I-8. Take Exit 78 (Spot Road) and turn right on Frontage Road. Drive approximately 1 mile and take a left (north) onto a dirt road (76 Ave. E) and drive another 7 miles. This road will end at a parking area where you will find information about local petroglyphs.

**Vehicle:** Two-wheel drive accessible, weather permitting.

**Contact:**
BLM
Phoenix Field Office
21605 N. 7$^{th}$ Ave
Phoenix, AZ 85027
Phone: 623-580-5500

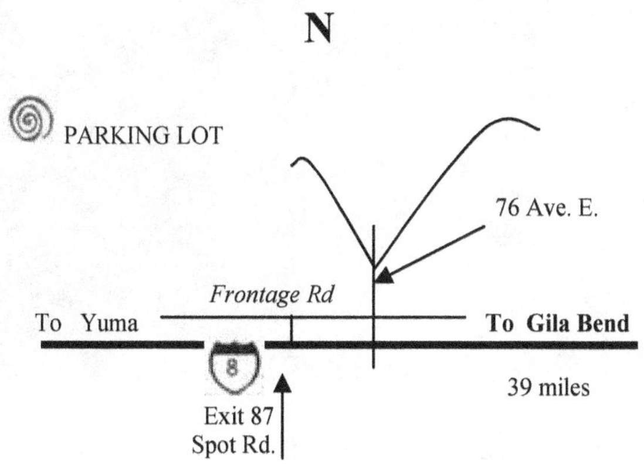

## Sipe White Mountain Wildlife Area

Sipe's 1,362 acres offer something for everyone. Bird watching is a favorite pastime; one might see a rare peregrine falcon, eagles, ospreys, hawks, wild turkeys, and several other species of birds. Additionally, elk, deer, and pronghorn antelope can be found throughout.

The visitor center has installed interpretive signs that describe the wildlife and the historic and prehistoric sites within the area.

The Pueblo people lived in this area farming and hunting. They built the Rudd Creek Pueblo, a pueblo style that was abundant around 1300 A.D.

Sipe White Mountain Wildlife Area provides a great learning experience for the entire family.

*Male figure with snakes?*

# Sipe White Mountain Wildlife Area Map

From Springerville Chamber of Commerce, drive toward Alpine following Hwy 191 south for 5 miles to Mile Marker 405. Turn right and drive on the gravel road for 5 miles until you reach the visitors center. You must sign in before going on the 2-mile round-trip hike on High Point Trail.

**Vehicle:** Two-wheel drive accessible.
**Contact:**
Pinetop Regional Office
2878 W. White Mountain
Pinetop AZ 85935
Phone: 928-367-4281

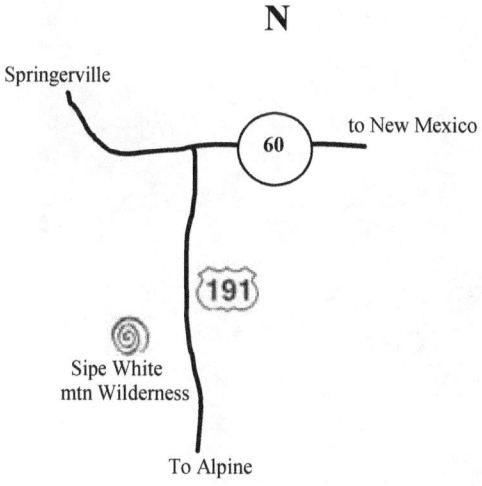

## Snake Gulch

At the mouth of Snake Gulch, there is a parking lot and an interpretation center dedicated to the history, rock art, and artifacts found throughout the gulch.

Snake Gulch has petroglyphs and pictographs. The pictographs have an array of colors and date back 2,000 years or more.

The V-shaped torsos seen below are typical Fremont Style (600 A.D. to about 1200 A.D.) and are found throughout Southern Utah. These "masterpieces of rock art" are found under overhangs, which offer protection from the elements.

*Dave and Margie Urquidi
In front of rock art.*

## Snake Gulch Map

Snake Gulch is located on the North Rim of the Grand Canyon and is managed by the Kaibab National Forest. This trip takes one into the Kanab-Utah wilderness. The nearest town is Jacob Lake. It is recommended that you camp in this area and drive to Snake Gulch. Jacob Lake offers RV camping, tent camping, gas, food and a motel.

This is a remote place, so let people know where you are going and pack plenty of water. This easy trail is 6 miles in and 6 miles out. It took us 6½ hours to complete the round trip. Watch out for snakes... the name speaks for itself.

The maps for this hike may be found at the Kaibab Plateau Visitors Center at Jacob Lake. For information, call 928-643-7298.

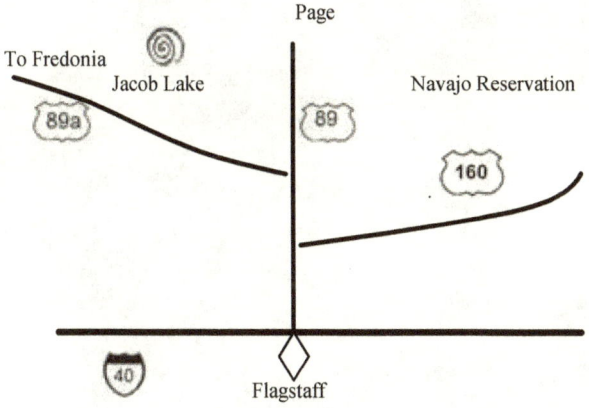

## South Fork

The Anasazi and Mogollon people co-existed in this area and left behind an abundance of rock art. The petroglyphs are along South Fork Road. They are eye level and can be seen from your car. The flute player is in the middle of the panel and is surrounded by clan signs. Some anthropologists think that the flute player, or Kokopelli, played the flute through their nose; this may explain the position of the flute.

Beautiful ponderosa pine trees surround the South Fork Campground, located at the end of this paved road. Primitive camping is available, however RVs are not recommended.

*Flute player surrounded by clan signs.*

# South Fork Map

From the town of Eagar, drive west on Hwy 260 for approximately 6 miles. Turn left at Mile Marker 391 onto South Fork Road and drive 1.4 miles to the petroglyphs on the west side of the road. The campgrounds are another 2.5 miles at the end of South Fork Road.
**(CAUTION: BEAR COUNTRY)**

**Vehicle:** Two-wheel drive accessible.

**Contact:**
Casa Malpais Archaeological Park and Museum
P.O. Box 807
318 E. Main Street
Springerville, AZ 85938
Phone: 928-333-5375

**N**

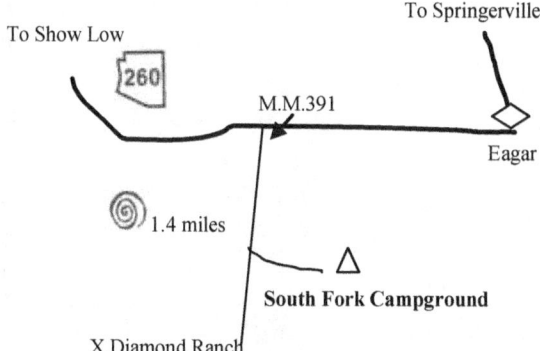

Guide to Rock Art Sites • 145

# South Mountain Park

South Mountain Park has 17,000 acres of mountain desert trails. Visitors must stay on all designated trails and are encouraged to carry plenty of water as temperatures can reach 120 degrees during the summer months.

The Hohokam rock art here is about 800 years old and there are more than 8,000 petroglyphs. Some of the rock art is located in Pima Canyon and Box Canyon. Look for the 14-mile National Trail on the western side of the park. The Holbert Trail is 2.5 miles, Geronimo Trail 1.4 miles, and the Desert Classic Trail is 9 miles. These trails are well marked with easy access for all hikers, although some areas are rocky and may be steep. Make sure you visit the interpretive center.

*Sunbursts, turtle and snake.*

# South Mountain Park Map

**Fee area: South Mountain will issue a map at the entrance**

From I-10, take Exit 155 (Baseline Road) and head west to Central Avenue and follow directions to the park.

**Contact:**
South Mountain Park
10919 S. Central Ave.
Phoenix, AZ 85040
Phone: 602-495-0222

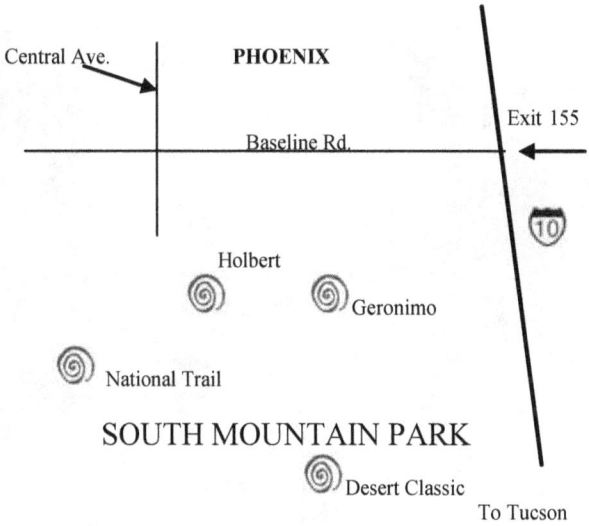

## Stanton Mining Town

"There's gold in them there hills!" It is said that more than 1,000,000.00 in gold and precious gemstones were taken out of this area back in the 1860's.

This was home to Charles Stanton, one of the richest men in Arizona, who was shot and killed at a nearby stagecoach stop. The Lost Dutchman Mining Association now owns Stanton Mining Town, loaded with Arizona history. They still allow visitors to tour some of the historical buildings.

There are several boulders just outside of town with petroglyphs that resemble Gila monsters.

*Lizard or Gila monster?*

# Stanton Mining Map

From Wickenburg, take 93 north to Hwy 89 and head north to the town of Congress. From Congress, drive north 2 miles to Stanton Road. Take a right and follow the gravel road for approximately 7 miles to Stanton. At Stanton, turn right and drive for 1.2 miles to an old rock dynamite building. The camp is an easy ¼ mile north. Follow the dry wash parallel to the dirt road.

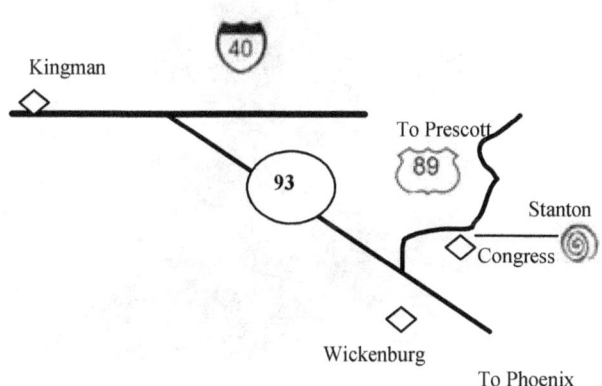

# Tyson Wells

In 1866 Quartzsite was just a stagecoach stop on the way to California. Now it's known for its famous rock and gem shows. More than a million visitors from all over the world come here for the Rock Pow Wow each year in the winter months.

The Patayan rock art is a little bit easier to find than gold. Tyson Tanks has petroglyphs and some caves. Although the rock art is fading and there is less of it, this is still an interesting place to visit.

*Petroglyphs near cave.*

# Tyson Wells Map

This sandy place is a four-wheel-drive area. The Bureau of Land Management manages Tyson Wells. Drive 7 miles south from Quartzsite on Hwy 95 to La Paz Valley Road. Turn right and drive about 1 mile and turn right on to Old Yuma Road. (No sign here)

(Drive 2.2 miles on this dirt road then turn left on a two-lane road and drive another ½ mile till you see the boulders and petroglyphs. Watch for snakes at this site.

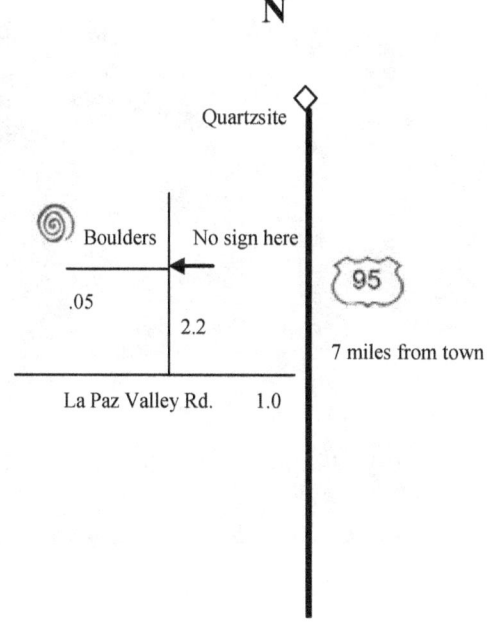

# V-Bar-V Ranch

   The V-Bar-V Ranch site is open to the public. The Coconino National Forest along with the Friends of the Forest manages this archaeological site. The Southern Sinagua people lived here from 1150 A.D. to 1400 A.D. They pecked turtles, crane-like figures, snakes and abstract figures into the rock.
   Early morning is the best time to photograph at this site. A fence protects the rock art and access is only during regular visiting hours. Please call for more information.

*Zoomorphic figures.*

## V-Bar-V Ranch Map

V-Bar-V Ranch is located 2.8 miles east of the junction of I-17 and S.R. 179 (F.R. 618). The entrance will be on your right, less than ½ mile past the Beaver Creek Campground. There will be a sign that reads: "V.V. Prehistoric Rock Art." The ranch is open Friday through Monday only.

**Vehicle:** Two-wheel drive accessible.

**Contact:**
Red Rock Ranger District
P.O. Box 20429
Sedona, AZ 86341
Phone: 928-282-4119

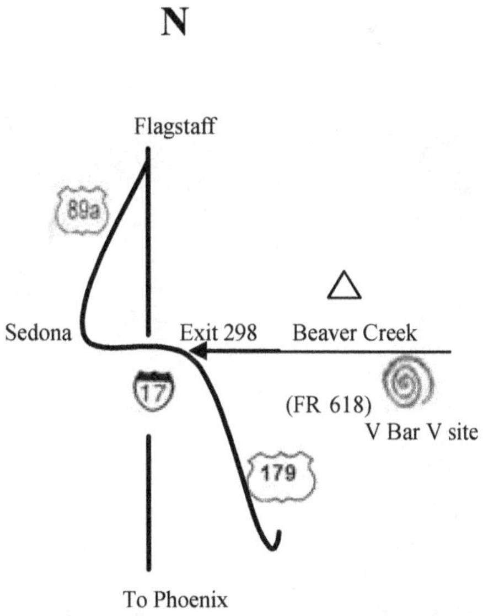

# Watch Tower

The Desert View Watch Tower was built to look like an Anasazi tower but on a much larger scale. Built in the 1930's as a gift shop, this large, round towering five-story building commands the best view of the canyon found anywhere in the state.

Once inside, the murals of rock art adorn the walls of the tower. They were done by a Hopi artist named Fred Kabotie, and represent the Hopi mythology and religious ceremonies. Artist Fred Greer's murals represent prehistoric pictographs and petroglyphs. They both made hundreds of copies of pictographs and petroglyphs with remarkable accuracy.

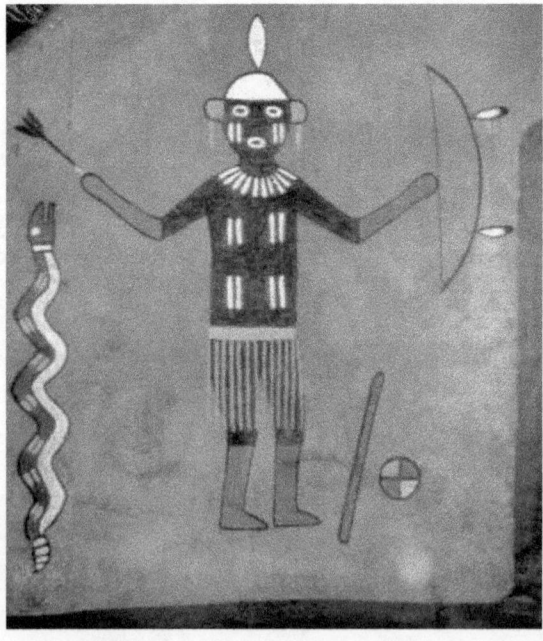

*Hopi mural.*

# Watch Tower Map

Watch Tower is located in the Grand Canyon. From the town of Williams, head north on Hwy 64 for approximately 55 miles. Pick up a map at the entrance to The Grand Canyon.

The Desert Watch Tower is located 25 miles east of the Grand Canyon entrance.

**Contact:**
Grand Canyon
National Park
P.O. Box 129
Grand Canyon, AZ
86023
Web Site: www.nps.gov/grca/

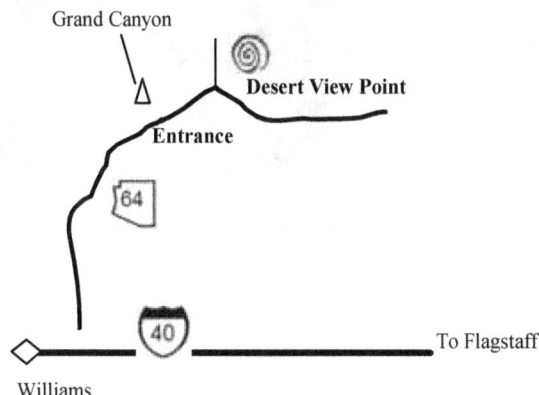

# Whipple Observatory

Petroglyphs were discovered on the site of the Whipple Observatory during its early construction. The Hohokam people may have etched these petroglyphs some 1,000 years ago.

Archaeoastronomy is the study of rock art that relates to solar observations. Early man looked to the stars and the sun to create calendars for their growing and harvest seasons. Could this rock art be a map of the stars? We will never know as this boulder was moved from its original location.

*Relocated petroglyph.*

# Whipple Observatory Map

The Whipple Observatory has a visitor center that exhibits natural science, astronomy, and cultural history displays.

From Tucson take Interstate 19 south 35 miles. Turn left (East) on Amado Monita Road and drive 10 miles to the observatory. Whipple is wheelchair accessible and has picnic tables and hiking trails.

**Vehicle:** Two-wheel drive accessible.

**Contact:**
Whipple Observatory
Box 97
Amado, AZ 85645
Phone: 520-670-5705

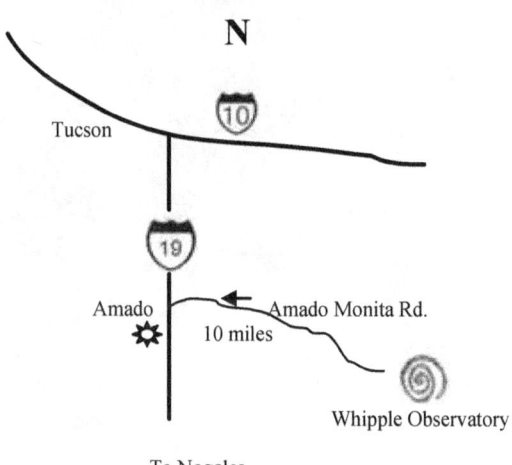

# White Tanks Regional Park
(Waterfall Canyon)

White Tanks Regional Park has hiking trails that will take you to hundreds of petroglyphs. This box canyon is an easy 1-mile hike from the trailhead. Most of the rock art in this area is Hohokam but some are believed to be of the Archaic culture dating back some 10,000 years. Other Petroglyphs are believed to be from the Paleo-Indians culture dating back some 8,000 years.

The goat camp trail is another short hike to some petroglyphs; most of the rock art is very accessible and the hike is geared to all levels.

*Large boulder full of abstract and geometric designs located at the park.*

# White Tanks Regional Park Map

From the West Valley of Phoenix, take Loop 101 to Olive Avenue (Exit 9). Drive west on Olive Avenue approximately 20 miles to the park entrance. Waterfall Canyon is located at White Tanks Regional Park. There may be an entrance fee.

**Vehicle:** Two-wheel drive accessible.

**Contact:**
White Tank Mountain Regional Park
13025 N. White Tank Mountain Road
Waddell, AZ 85355
Phone: 623-935-2505
Web site: www.maricopa.gov/parks/white_tank/

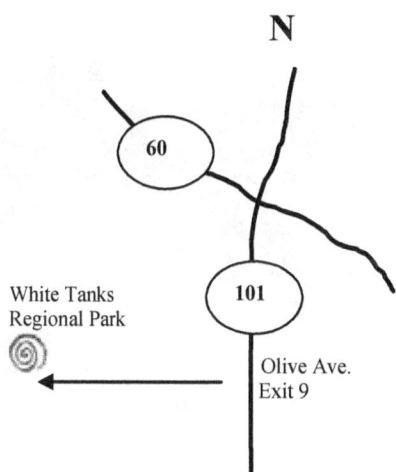

## Wupatki National Monument

The Crack-in-Rock excursion is a weekend backpack trip of about 14 to 16 miles. Bring your own gear, food, water, etc. This trip is by lottery as they only take few people at a time. A fee is required when the reservation is confirmed.

Crack-in-Rock is a Hopi Pueblo located on top of a mesa along with several petroglyphs. The two-day hike takes you through historic and prehistoric sites that are interpreted by a Wupatki staff member. The hike is not for the faint of heart; you pack it in and you pack it out, and that means all personal hygiene items as well.

Happy trails!

*One of many Wupatki petroglpyhs found throughout the monument.*

# Wupatki National Monument Map

Drive approximately 15 miles north of Flagstaff on Hwy 89. Follow signs to Wupatki (Sunset Crater).

**Vehicle:** RV parking available at Bonita Creek Campground.

**Contact:**
Wupatki National Monument
6400 N. Highway 89
Flagstaff, AZ 86004
Phone: 928-679-2365

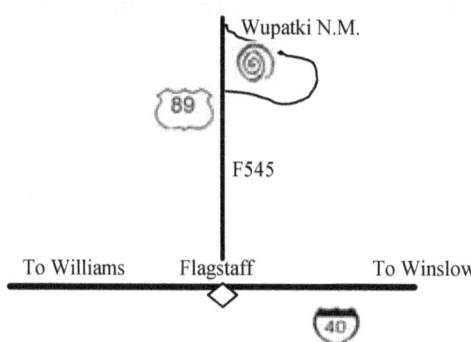

# Bibliography

**Anderson, Keith. 1971.**
Excavations at Betatakin, Kiet Siel. *Kiva.*

**Barnes, F.A. and Michaelene Pendleton. 1979.**
*Canyon Country Prehistoric Indians: Cultures, Ruins, Artifacts and Rock Art.* Wasatch Publishers, Inc, Salt Lake City.

**Benson, Phil. 1989.**
*Native American Petroglyphs: Along the Trail.* Las Vegas Southern Nevada Times Publishing.

**Bicknell, Robin S. 2001.**
*Images from the Past.* Patrice Press, Tucson.

**Bilbo, Michael and Kay Sutherland. 1986.**
*Stylistic Evolution of Rock Art in the Jornada Region.*

**Brew, J.O. 1979.**
*American Indians V-9.* A. Ortiz, ed. Smithsonian, Washington, D.C.

**Brody, J.J. 1990.**
*The Anasazi.* Rizzoli, New York.

**Cole, Sally J. 1990.**
*Legacy on Stone: Rock Art of the Colorado Plateau and Four Corners Region.* Johnson Books, Boulder.

**Crosby, Harry. 1997.**
*The Cave Painting of Baja California, 2$^{nd}$ Ed.*
Sunbelt Publishing, El Cajon, California.

**DiPeso Charles C. 1974.**
*Casa Grandes: A Fallen Trading Center of the Gran Chichimeca.* Amerind Foundation, Dragoon, Arizona.

**Driver, H.E. 1961.**
*Indians of North America.* University of Chicago Press, Chicago.

**Frazier, Kendrick. 1986.**
People of Chaco: A Canyon and Its Culture. W.W. Norton, New York.

**Grant, Campbell. 1992.**
*Rock Art of the American Indian.* Vista Books, Dillon, Colorado.

**Grant, Campbell. 1978.**
*Canyon DeChelly, Its People and Rock Art.*
University of Arizona Press.

**Haury, Emil W. 1976.**
*The Hohokam: Desert Farmers and Craftsmen. Excavations at Snaketown, Arizona.* University of Arizona Press, Tucson.

**Hedges, Ken. 1981.**
Phosphenes in the Context of Native American Rock Art. The American Rock Art, Vols. VII, VIII. F. G. Bock, ed.

**Heizer, R.F. and M.A.Baumhoff. 1962.**
*Prehistoric Rock Art of Nevada and Eastern California.* University of California Press, Berkeley.

**Hibben, F.C. 1975.**
*Kiva Art of the Anasazi.* KC Publications, Las Vegas.

**James, Janetsky &Vlasich. 1981.**
*Prehistory, Ethnohistory and History of Eastern Nevada.* BLM Cultural Resource Series.

**Jennings, Jesse D. 1978.**
Prehistory of Utah and the Eastern Great Basin. *Anthropological Papers No. 98.* University of Utah, Salt Lake City.

**Johnson, Clay. 1992.**
Methodology for Identifying, Observing, Recording and Reporting Solar Interactive Rock Art Panels. *Annual Symposium of the Utah Rock Art Research Association, Utah.*

**Lucius W.A. 1976.**
Archaeological Investigation in the Maze District, Canyon Lands National Park, Utah. *Antiquities Section Selected Papers, Vol. 3 No. 11.* Utah State Historical Society.

**Martineau, LaVan. 1994.**
*The Rocks Begin to Speak.* KC Publications, Las Vegas.

**Muench, M. David, and Polly Schaafsma. 1995.**
*Images in Stone.* Brown Trout Publishers, San Francisco.

**Noble, David G. 2000.**
*Ancient Ruins of the Southwest.* Northland Publishing, Flagstaff.

**Nordenskiold, G. E. 1979.**
*The Cliff Dwellers of the Mesa Verde.* Rio Grande Press.

**Patterson, Alex. 1992.**
*A Field Guide to Rock Art Symbols of the Greater Southwest.* Johnson Books, Boulder.

**Pike & Muench. 1974.**
*Anasazi.* American West Publishing.

**Reichard, Gladys. 1950.**
*A Navajo Religion: A study of Symbolism.* Stratford Press, New York.

**Robin, Arthur H. & Lisa & William Ferguson. 1989.**
*Rock Art of Bandelier National Monument.* University of New Mexico Press, Albuquerque.

**Schaafsma, Polly. 1994.** *The Rock Art of Utah.* University of Utah Press, Salt Lake City.

**Slifer, Dennis & James Duffield. 1994**
Kokopell: *Flute Player Images in Rock Art.* Santa Fe, N.M. Ancient City Press,

# Glossary

**Abraded** - term used to described an artificially smoothed surface on which rock art was placed.

**Abstract image** - an image that cannot be readily identified even though it possesses a clear and definite form.

**Anthropology** - the social science that examines human culture and experience, past and present.

**Anthropomorphic image** - an image resembling a human figure or a recognizable human part, such as a hand or foot.

**Anasazi** - a culture living between 300 B.C.–1300 A.D.

**Archaeoastronomy** - the anthropology of astronomy; reconstruction of past astronomical practices, including celestial lore, religion mythologies, and how ancient cultures related to the sky.

**Archaeology** - the sub-field of anthropology that examines past human culture through the excavation and analysis of material remains.

**Archaic-** Eastern Archaic tradition is an archaeological time period from about 6000 B.C. to 800 B.C. It is characterized as a small community supported mainly by hunting and gathering of natural resources.

**Atlatl** - a stick with a hook on the end used to throw a spear or dart.

**Combination rock art** - rock art that is pecked or engraved that has painting added.

**Culture** - a community that characterize the life of particular beliefs, knowledge, and behaviors.

**Finger painting** - a technique for producing pictographs in which the finger is used to apply paint to rock surfaces or walls.

**Geoglyph** - images formed on the ground by scraping away surface material to form an image out of the exposed soil or by arranging stones to form a figure such as a petroform.

**Geometric image** - An image depicting an identifiable shape, such as a circle, oval, square, spiral, rectangle, etc.

**Glyphs** - short for petroglyphs.

**Graph** - short for pictograph.

**Hohokam** - a culture living between 300 B.C.–1300 A.D.

**Intaglio** - large ground drawings created by removing the pebbles that make up desert pavement. Intaglios are usually in the outline of animals (zoomorphs) or human-like figures (anthropomorphs). Also known as geoglyphs.

**Mogollon culture** – a culture living between 300 B.C. and 1100 A.D.

**Motif** - an image or design, such as a handprint or a sunburst.

**Patination** - the thin layer of material that forms on a rock surface after weathering that can change its color (patina).

**Patayan** - (meaning old people) is used by archaeologists to describe prehistoric and historic Native American cultures between A.D. 700–1550.

**Pecked** - a dimple appearance on stone when a hammer stone or deer horn is used to shape or roughen a surface.

**Petroform** - a representational figure laid out on the ground with stones or boulders.

**Petroglyphs** - an image carved or pecked into or incised into a rock surface.

**Pictograph** - images that are painted onto a rock surface.

**Pigment** - the colored substance, usually a mineral, that can be mixed with a binder to create paint.

**Polychrome** - having two or more colors.

**Prehistory** - before written history.

**Rock art** – images carved, drawn, or painted onto rock surfaces or walls.

**Rock varnish** – microscopically thin layers composed of materials or weather-drawn dust that build up on rock surfaces.

**Shaman** – a religious specialist, one who has healing powers, who performs rituals designed to communicate with the spirit world.

**Sinagua** – an Arizona prehistoric Puebloan culture that lived in the Flagstaff and Verde Valley, also thought to be related to the Anasazi.

**Yuman** – a language derived from the people living along the Colorado River.

**Zoomorphic image** – an image that represents an animal figure, a recognizable animal, or animal track.

# Resources
# &
# Places to Visit in Arizona

*Note: Phone numbers, addresses, and other information listed here are subject to change.*

**Arizona Archaeological Council**
P.O. Box 27566
Tempe, AZ 85285
Phone: 520-523-7044
Web site: http://www.arizonaarchaeologicalcouncil.org/

**Arizona Archaeological and Historical Society**
Arizona State Museum
P.O. Box 210026
Tucson, AZ 85721
Phone: 520-621-6302
Web site: http://www.statemuseum.arizona.edu/about/visit.shtml

**Arizona Rock Art Research Association**
Arizona State museum
P.O. Box 210026
Tucson, AZ 85721
Phone: 520-621-3999
Web site: www.arara.org

**Arizona Heard Museum**
2301 N. Central Ave
Phoenix, AZ 85004
Phone: 602-252-8848
Web site: http://www.heard.org/NETCOMMUNITY/

**Arizona Museum for Youth**
35 N. Robson
Mesa, AZ
Phone: 480-644-2467
Web site: http://www.arizonamuseumforyouth.com/Home.aspx

**Deer Valley Rock Art center**
3711 W. Deer Valley Road
Glendale, AZ 85308
Phone: 623-582- 8007
Web site: http://www.asu.edu/clas/shesc/dvrac/

**Hoo-Hoogam Ki Museum**
10005 East Osborn Road
Scottsdale, AZ 85256
Phone: 480-850-8190
Web site: http://www.srpmic.com

**Northern Arizona Museum**
3101 N. Ft. Valley Road
Flagstaff, AZ 86001
Phone: 928-774-5213
Web site: http://www.musnaz.org/

**Pueblo Grande Museum
and Archaeological Park**
4619 W. Washington St.
Phoenix, AZ 85034
Phone: 602-495-0901
Web site: http://phoenix.gov/parks/pueblo.html

**Bureau Of Land Management
Arizona State Office
One North Central Avenue Suite 800
Phoenix, AZ 85004-4427**

| Arizona Strip District | Colorado River District | Gila District | Phoenix District |
|---|---|---|---|
| **AZ Strip** Field Office 345 East Riverside Drive St. George, UT 84790 Phone: 435-688-3200<br><br>Vermillion Cliffs National Monument<br><br>Grand Canyon Parashant National Monument | **Lake Havasu** Field Office 2610 Sweetwater Ave. Lake Havasu City, AZ 86406 Phone: 928-505-1200<br><br>**Kingman** Field Office 2755 Mission Blvd Kingman, AZ 86409 Phone: 928-718-3761<br><br>**Yuma** Field Office 2555 East Gila ridge | **Sierra Vista** 1763 Paseo San Luis Sierra Vista, AZ 85635 Phone 520-439-6400<br><br>**Safford** 711 14$^{th}$ Ave. Safford, AZ 85546 Phone: 928-348-4400<br><br>**Tucson** 12661 East Broadway Tucson, AZ 85748 Phone: 520-258-7238 | **Phoenix** Field Office 21604 N. 7$^{th}$ Ave. Phoenix, AZ 85027 Phone: 623-580-5500<br><br>For<br><br>Hassayampa<br><br>Aqua Fria National Monument<br><br>Lower Sonoran<br><br>Sonoran Desert National Monument |

# National Parks/ Monuments

**Web site**: www.nps.gov

**Canyon De Chelly National Monument**
P.O. Box 588
Chinle, AZ 86503
928-674-5500

**Casa Grande Ruins National Monument**
1100 West Ruins Drive
Coolidge, AZ 85228
520-723-317

**Grand Canyon National Park**
P.O. Box 129
Grand Canyon, AZ 86023
928-638-7888

**Montezuma Castle National Monument**
P.O. Box 219
Camp Verde, AZ 86322
Visitor Center
928-567-3322
Park Headquarters
928-567-5276

**Organ Pipe Cactus National Monument**
10 Organ Pipe Drive
Ajo, AZ 85321
520-387-6849

**Pipe Springs National Monument**
HC 65 Box 5
Fredonia, AZ 86022
Main Office
928-643-7105

**Saguaro National Park**
3693 South Old Spanish Trail
Tucson, AZ 85730
520-733-5153

**Sunset Crater National Monument**
Route 3 Box 149
Flagstaff, AZ 86004
928-526-0502

**Tonto National Monument**
HC 02 Box 4602
Roosevelt, AZ 85545
928-467-2241

**Tuzigoot National Monument**
P.O. Box 219
Camp Verde, AZ 86322
Visitor Information
928-634-5564

**Walnut Canyon National Monument**
6400 N. Hwy 89
Flagstaff, AZ 86004
Headquarters, Flagstaff Area National Monuments
928-526-1157
Walnut Canyon National Monument Visitor Center
928-526-3367

**Wupatki National Monument**
Flagstaff Area National Monuments
6400 N. Hwy 89
Flagstaff, AZ 86004
Headquarters, Flagstaff Area National Monuments
928-526-1157
Wupatki National Monument Visitor Center
928-679-2365

# Cities and Towns

In alphabetical order to locate nearby rock art

| City or Towns | Pages |
|---|---|
| Ajo | 38,108 |
| Alpine | 24,140 |
| Apache Junction | 36,48,64,146,158 |
| Arivaca | 90 |
| Ash Fork | 114 |
| Benson | 44 |
| Bisbee | 52,100 |
| Black Canyon City | 18,20 |
| Bouse | 26 |
| Bullhead City | 72,76 |
| Cave Creek | 36,48,146,158 |
| Chinle | 30 |
| Chloride | 40 |
| Cottonwood | 112,152 |
| Cortez Junction | 18,20 |
| Eagar | 32,74,96,140,144 |
| Flagstaff | 22,28,78,92,102,112,120, 152,154,160 |
| Fredonia | 42,94,106,142 |
| Gila Bend | 38,56,110,138 |
| Grand Canyon | 28,120 |
| Harcuvar | 62 |
| Heber | 124 |
| Holbrook | 88,118,134 |
| Jacob Lake | 42,94,106,142 |

# Cities and Towns
In alphabetical order to locate nearby rock art

| City or Towns | Pages |
|---|---|
| Kayenta | 22,30,104 |
| Kingman | 40,72,76,80 |
| Lake Havasu City | 86 |
| Overgaard | 124 |
| Page | 58,104 |
| Parker | 26,62,86 |
| Patagonia | 116 |
| Payson | 124 |
| Phoenix | 36,48,64,136,146,148,158 |
| Prescott | 18,20,126,148 |
| Quartzsite | 26,62,110,150 |
| Safford | 46,54,60 |
| Salome | 62 |
| Sedona | 112,152 |
| Show Low | 32,66,74,96,124,144 |
| Sierra Vista | 52,100 |
| Springerville | 32,66,74,124,144 |
| St. Johns | 74,96 |
| Tombstone | 44,52,100 |
| Tuba City | 22,102 |
| Tucson | 34,50,82,84,96,116,122, 136,156 |
| Wellton | 16,98,110,138 |
| Wickenburg | 26,62,110,132,148 |
| Wilcox | 46,54,60 |
| Williams | 28,78,92,114,120,154,160 |
| Winslow | 68,88,118,124,134 |
| Yuma | 16,98,110,138 |

# About the Author

Robin Scott Bicknell, an archaeologist for more than thirty years, has dedicated his life to the study of the Native Americans' way of living. His passion for photographing rock art has inspired others to become involved in both the appreciation and preservation of this national heritage

Mr. Bicknell is a member of the Deer Valley Rock Art Center and the American Rock Art Research Association. He has recorded rock art with Dr. Clemens W. Meighan, Professor of Anthropology, University of California Los Angeles, for the **UCLA Rock Art Archives**. His name **"Robin 1"** is recorded in the San Diego Archives for a Native American site found during one of his surveys.

Bicknell is a Vietnam veteran and has been a member of the Veterans of Foreign Wars (VFW) for the past thirty years. He is also a member of an organization called E Clampus Vitus (ECV). Established by miners around the 1850's to protect their widows and orphans, ECV today still follows their tradition as well as contributes to the recovery of the history of Arizona and the western United States.

During his travels through the American Southwest and Mexico, Bicknell has taken a special interest photographing not only rock art but also landscapes and ghost towns. He has photographed with instructor Al Weber, a friend and colleague of Ansel Adams, who he taught with at Yosemite for eighteen years.

Bicknell is a well-known artist, exhibiting in many galleries and stores throughout the nation and abroad. His artwork consists of two types:

**Rock Art** - Hand etched replicas of petroglyphs in sandstone rock. The images are photographed at the original sites and carry documentation of the area where they are located.

**Photographs** - Photos of both petroglyphs and pictographs are taken from the original sites mentioned in this book and from his previous book, *Images from the Past: A Self-Guided Tour of Petroglyphs and Pictographs of the American Southwest*.

# IMAGES FROM THE PAST

## A Self-Guided Tour of Petroglyphs and Pictographs of the American Southwest

The Anasazi, Hohokam, and other prehistoric cultures left behind virtually indelible reminders of their existence, popularly known as rock art. The examples probably number in the thousands in the American Southwest alone, but most people are aware of only a few specimens. How to reach them and how to admire the handiwork of people who have been dead for a millennium, has been a daunting task. Robin Scott Bicknell has provided explicit driving (and hiking) directions to forty-seven of the best sites in the states of Arizona, New Mexico, Nevada, Utah, California and Texas, as well as Baja Mexico. In most cases the motorist can follow the site maps and drive to within a few feet of the rock art, while others require a short hike.

The thrills await us all! Get behind the wheel and drive into the past. See the legacy of those who were here centuries before the arrival of Columbus.

# BOOK REVIEWS

**Tombstone Epitaph Tombstone Arizona**
At first glance, the reader will realize that such a book as this, is long overdue. Another reason that such a production is vital is that it will not be many

years before all this ancient art will have disappeared. Therefore, the 47 photographs that are included are a real treasure.
—Ben T. Traywick

Bicknell does not attempt to decipher the messages left behind, nor does he delve into the mysteries of these great peoples now lost in the obscurity of time. Bicknell takes his pleasure in the simplicity of visiting these outdoor galleries and photographing the ancient artwork.

In *Images from the Past*, it is easy to discern Bicknell's respect for the sites he has explored and photographed. He hopes to engender this respect in all visitors, so that they may learn to "take nothing but pictures, leave nothing but footprints."
—Cortez Newspaper, Cortez Colorado


To order our books online go to
WWW.BOOKS.BY/ROCKINROBIN

# Important Numbers to Report Vandalism

Arizona Game & Fish    800-826-3257

National Park Service    800-227-7286

## 1-800-Vandals

**For more information on the Grand Canyon State:**

http://www.arizonaguide.com/

**Arizona Tourism Office:** 800-842-8257